Gewers Pudewill

TAILOR MADE

Architecture

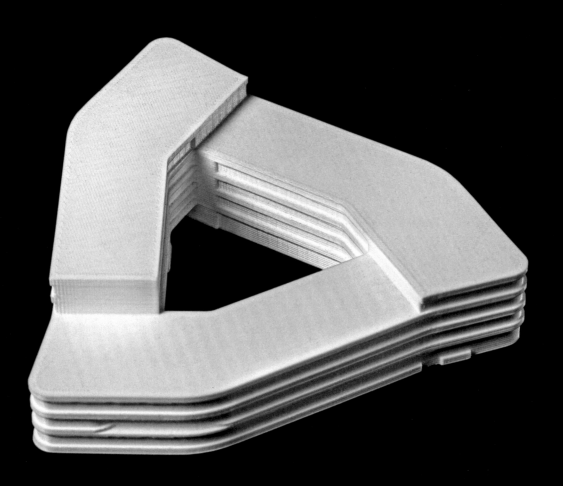

Gewers Pudewill

TAILOR MADE

Architecture

PARK BOOKS

Tailor-made—Wide-ranging, but nevertheless distinctive

The œuvre of Gewers Pudewill encompasses buildings for an astonishingly broad range of functions and locations. Common to all of them is high quality down to the last detail, and the conviction that new commissions require new solutions—from the grand-scale perspective of the building's urban context, all the way to its interior design.
Whether the task is to transform a disused department store from the GDR era into a new hotspot for the digital economy or plan a new Berlin headquarters for one of the world's major music companies, or whether a major internet fashion retailer wants to build a high-rise in Berlin with spaces where employees can mingle and enjoy views and open-air terraces on the upper stories, too—Gewers Pudewill always respond with solutions tailored to the site, function and challenge.
Although a number of hallmark strands run through their work, the two architects never repeat their successes in formulaic fashion, but compose an individual response to each new commission.
In this book, Gewers Pudewill's approaches and solutions can be seen and compared for the first time in one place, in a selection ranging from a senior center in Brandenburg to a biotech facility on the Rostock waterfront to the headquarters of a local utility company in Regensburg—and much more besides.
These high-quality designs, presented here for the first time in images and texts, testify to the fact that success, far from making the architects rest on their laurels, acts upon them as an incentive. It is sometimes the boldness and verve of a sculptor, sometimes the expertise of a building professional that makes these designs and buildings what they are: sensitive urban building blocks and delightful neighbors in the metropolis, or new buildings forging identities in rural areas or on the peripheries of towns and cities.
While other contemporary architects become set on developing a recognizable, always replicable signature style, which caters to the needs of a building commission only to a greater or lesser extent, Gewers Pudewill prefer to devote their time, attention and

energy to designing details and aesthetics appropriate to steel, glass, stone, plaster and other construction materials. This includes load-bearing structures and floor plans that do not place a strait-jacket on operating and functional processes, but on the contrary make life (and not just working life) in the buildings easier. Gewers Pudewill's more recent buildings are characterized in some cases by the crystalline expression of black-framed glass or mutually offset stories, in others by the smoothly rounded, blonde brick corners of an apartment building in the heart of Berlin's newspaper district. This many-sidedness is demonstrated quite literally by the high-rise on the Spree: the exterior walls fold alternately inwards and outwards on each story, creating terraces and a play of recesses and projections. The headquarters of a family concern in Hamburg's HafenCity, meanwhile, is at once rooted in its Hanseatic setting and an expression of the firm's global business activities. Bold openings in the brick building create wide terraces with views of the Elbe.

Residential and office complexes may be the primary types of buildings commissioned from architects in Germany today, but Gewers Pudewill also design for research and industry. They know how to lend elegance to laboratories on the outskirts of towns or at motorway intersections, for example, and how to create an effect with exterior facades that references the work being pursued inside the institute. It may be a bright-white building that stands for innovation, research and ceramics, with a facade of fine-grained horizontal bands of ceramic material, or it may be a research center for white goods, modular in composition and with dynamic curves in its metal facade, alluding to the domestic-appliance technology being developed and tested in-house. The designs by Gewers Pudewill are preceded by detailed analyses, and by the practical optimization of workflows and in some cases complex interrelationships between functions and spaces, in order to arrive at solutions that are customized for every new commission —in other words, tailor-made!

ULF MEYER

The role of the designer is to be a very good, thoughtful host anticipating the needs of his guests.

CHARLES EAMES

Sur/faces

Backstage

Foreword 4

Berlin, Berlin 22

UP! 30
Stream 38
NeuHouse 54
Im Wirtschaftswunder 62
European headquarters of the Sony Music Group 64
Berlin Brandenburg Airport Willy Brandt, service buildings 68
Linienstrasse 74
B/S/H/ Bosch und Siemens Hausgeräte Technology Center 76
Mercedes-Benz Sales Organization Germany 80

Spaces for People 90

Mercedes-Benz Sales Organization Germany, Berlin 94
"Regine Hildebrandt" Senior Center, Bernau 96
Marquard & Bahls, Hamburg 100
NeuHouse, Berlin 106
Columbiadamm, Berlin 108
Prinzenviertel, Berlin 110
Treskowallee, Berlin 112
Linienstrasse, Berlin 114
Wohnpark Joachimstrasse/Lindenstrasse, Berlin 116
Andreashöfe, Berlin 120
Villa, Potsdam 124
DSTRCT, Berlin 126
Volkswagen Head Office Building, Wolfsburg 134
REWAG, Regensburg 136

Context 140

REWAG, Regensburg 144
Volkswagen Head Office Building, Wolfsburg 152
Marquard & Bahls, Hamburg 160
Fraunhofer IKTS, Hermsdorf 164
Columbiadamm, Berlin 168
DSTRCT, Berlin 170
Fraunhofer IPA, Stuttgart 184
Centogene, Rostock 188

Sur/faces 198

Centogene, Rostock 202
NeuHouse, Berlin 204
UP!, Berlin 206
Franklinstrasse, Berlin 210
B/S/H/ Bosch und Siemens Hausgeräte Technology Center, Berlin 212
Fraunhofer IKTS, Hermsdorf 214
Marquard & Bahls, Hamburg 216
European headquarters of the Sony Music Group 220
German Federal Institute for Risk Assessment, Berlin 221
Carl Zeiss Meditec, Berlin 222
Columbiadamm, Berlin 224
Linienstrasse, Berlin 226
Villa, Potsdam 228
Fraunhofer IPA, Stuttgart 230
Berlin Brandenburg Airport Willy Brandt, service buildings, Berlin 232
Stream, Berlin 234
REWAG, Regensburg 236
Im Wirtschaftswunder, Berlin 238
Stream, Berlin 240
Mercedes-Benz Sales Organization Germany, Berlin 242

Backstage 247

Team 2008–2023 258

Acknowledgements 272
Image credits 272
Imprint 272

The tower is the opposite of an ivory tower.

HENRY PUDEWILL ON THE STREAM BUILDING

Berlin, Berlin

The Berlin buildings
by Gewers Pudewill
are a contribution to
the city's new shape

In the years following the turn of the millennium, architecture and urban planning in Berlin were characterized by a confrontation between two camps: on the one hand, architects who were willing to accommodate themselves to the conservative postmodern views of Hans Stimmann, the Berlin Senate's director of construction, and on the other, "independent" practices more or less openly opposed to this stance. When Gewers Pudewill was founded in 2008, it did well not to align itself with either of these two factions. The office—due to the biographies of its two founders—had its roots neither in Steinernes Berlin ("Stony Berlin"—a policy of cladding Berlin buildings in sandstone) nor in the thinking behind the Planwerk Innenstadt. But nor did it belong to the type of two-partner offices making up the opposition, such as Barkow/Leibinger, Sauerbruch/Hutton, Augustin/Ernst, Grüntuch/Ernst and Chestnutt/Niess. Instead, its most important sources of inspiration lay in sculpture and the British high-tech architecture of the 1990s (Gewers) and in industrial building and programming (Pudewill). These—ideologically not connoted—positions allowed the two architects to look at and design for the city with a fresh eye and approach. From being the stronghold of techno and an East-West metropolis in the "wild 90s," Berlin had by this time developed into a center of the new Europe, an amplified EU, a start-up location, a magnet for the digital economy and a center of attraction for young people from all over the world.

Workspace for the digital economy

The "new Berlin" is embodied most clearly by the UP! building >30. Following a radical conversion and remodeling project, a former GDR department store in Friedrichshain was transformed into a modern workspace for the digital economy. Designed together with Jasper Architects, the concept envisaged opening up the department-store "box." The existing building, with its enormous ceiling heights and wide grid of supports, lent itself to conversion. Today, UP! houses modern working environments with inspiring, shabby chic interiors that go well with the new (and old) Berlin. The concept of the "digital extension of physical rooms" allows for "non-determined workspaces" that are used flexibly in new ways every day, and which thrive on their relationship to outdoor space: the architects call these informal workspaces "non-territorial office worlds." Through the addition of three stories, it was possible to compensate for the areas of floor lost due to the incisions in the ground plan. The four large circulation cores were retained and supplemented by a fifth elevator tower. Hastened by the pandemic and the boom in online trade, further department stores in Berlin will likely fall into disuse. The conversion of the department store next to Ostbahnhof railway station offers a model of how to respond. As an example of the revitalization of unused commercial real estate, the UP! building is of great interest to other cities, too.

Digital natives

With their Stream office tower >38 for the same client and user, Gewers Pudewill have provided the Mediaspree district—Berlin's most important area of urban renewal—with a literal and figurative high point. The Stream building carries ideas for a new office and working environment for digital natives to new heights, by linking interior and exterior spaces and the floors in ways that have never been seen before in high-rise construction. As a sculpture in the urban landscape in front of the neighboring multifunctional arena, the 24 stories alternately project and recede like angular folds, in order to allow spaces for communication and views over the ever-growing city. For the first time, the distinctive form goes further than an "extrusion" that simply multiplies the surface area of the building site, as is common in modernist high-rise construction.
Berlin has a weak subsoil and no topographical features to limit its expansion. As a consequence, the development of skyscrapers in the twentieth century passed it by. Since the turn of the millennium,

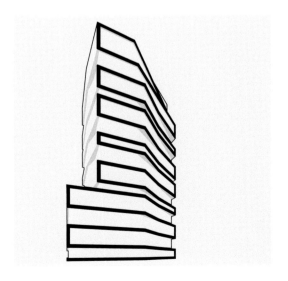

Berlin has been trying to catch back up with commercial high-rise construction. Even if local politicians delight in capping high-rise buildings and only grant permission for stumps, seeing them as being "more compatible with the city," medium-height skyscrapers have sprung up into the skies over Berlin. The Mediaspree business and entertainment district is marked by a total of six high-rises. The Stream is the most striking of these, because it is no ordinary tower block, but one vast sculpture: terraces tapering to a point make the building appear as if it were an uneven stack of 24 floors. The pleated form with its alternately projecting stories lends the tower its contours. In this way, the mass and width of the structure are articulated. The form is not an end in itself, however: the aim was to create "room for inspiration and communication." This goal is achieved through two innovations in high-rise construction: first, the terraces on each story, some of which wrap around two corners, and second, the internal flights of stairs, doubling as seating, that each connect two floors and break the flat layering of uncoupled stories in high-rise construction. The eight staircases at two different locations in the ground plan are finished with oak surfaces, making them a pleasure to sit on. The "fluid spatial continuum" across the stories fosters a friendly working atmosphere. All workstations and conference rooms enjoy sweeping views of the city and its River Spree—the "Stream." Once the EDGE East Side office tower on Warschauer Brücke, designed by Copenhagen architects BIG, is completed, an online retailer from the USA will be occupying 28 of its 35 floors. The two office towers—as home to rival companies—will thus proclaim the age of online commerce on the Berlin skyline.

The architects won the competition with a tower on an irregular hexagonal ground plan, which arose from the course of a footpath leading to the area in front of the arena. The building regulations allowed the site to be fully developed; in other words, they did not stipulate more slender proportions for the tower. The development plan gave the building volume little leeway, but the layering, folding and offsetting of the stories was a skillful means of creating a more complex building. The tower marks the entrance from the direction of the Oberbaum-City district. The lower seven stories form a boot-shaped plinth in the height and style of Berlin's perimeter-block development. The strongly defined "roofline" edge, which the neighboring buildings also follow, was a stipulation of the design. The tower grows out of the block. Its height of 65 meters is broken up by slanting angles. The "folding of the ceilings upwards" and the resulting offset stories create room everywhere for attractive roof terraces. The narrower side of the tower overlooks the arena, while the longer side faces towards the Spree. Where the tower rises from its base, there is a large rooftop terrace. A beacon of the Mediaspree quarter, the Stream office tower introduces two innovations in high-rise construction that help create an attractive working environment for the digital native generations.

Starry skies

From the Stream office tower, the view looking west falls on the black-and-glass facade of the headquarters of the sales organization >80 of a well-known car manufacturer. Just as the Mercedes-Benz star on top of the Europa-Center was a landmark of West Berlin in the years before reunification, the company's circular symbol now shines above the new Mühlenstrasse quarter, which stands for Berlin's reinvention of its econo-

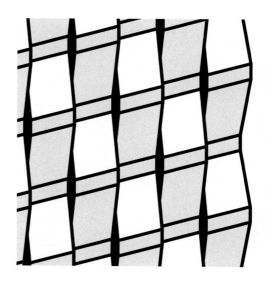

my in the internet age. The high-rise on the Spree is accompanied by three rectangular blocks. Although the sales headquarters is considerably shorter than the Europa-Center near the Kaiser Wilhelm Memorial Church, its more interesting facade makes it a commanding symbol of urban development on the Spree. The interplay between the cubic buildings and the rhythmically structured glass is charged with tension. Due to the zig-zag "folds" of the horizontally offset window panes, light is reflected similar to the way it is from a prism. This crystalline effect in turn reflects technical precision.

At the gateway to the world

In the case of the residential building that Gewers Pudewill designed near the Jewish Museum, mineral materials were chosen for the facades. Thus a light-colored clinker brick is used for the apartment complex on Enckestrasse, and likewise for its pendant on Columbiadamm, where it mirrors the facades of Tempelhof Airport opposite. In terms of material, color and roofline height, the Columbiadamm urban living complex is oriented towards the famous terminal designed by Ernst Sagebiel—a milestone of early airport construction and an important memorial to Berlin's early postwar history.

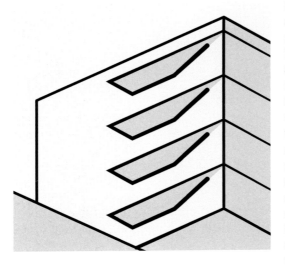

In terms of urban development, the residential complex on Columbiadamm >108 completes the neighboring quarter of co-housing communities. Upholding the traditional Berlin mix of retail and living units, a continuous base story connects the apartment building with the commercial wing. The two structures are laid out around an inner courtyard, likewise in typical Berlin fashion. The glazed *bel étage* and its undercut lend the building its sculptural air. Narrow, light-colored and semi-transparent cladding elements give the elevations their tranquil elegance and aesthetically link all parts of the building into a harmonious whole.

The Columbiadamm complex lies opposite the airport and next to the Columbiahalle, as an extension of the administrative buildings on Platz der Luftbrücke. As already mentioned, it takes account of these surroundings in its materials, color and roofline height. The proximity of the Columbiahalle event venues was another consideration. Thus the base story running unbroken between the apartment building and the commercial block serves as a noise barrier. Above it, the gap between the residential and commercial halves of the complex allows the structures to be individually perceived and ensures that light passes through into the inner courtyard. The complex blends sensitively into its context despite its size, and forms a keystone of the development on this side of Columbiadamm.

The NeuHouse >54 on Fromet-und-Moses-Mendelssohn-Platz is likewise located near an architectural landmark. Here, too, the project was to design a building that would complete a new quarter—and, moreover, to skillfully marry this new complex with a listed building, one of Kreuzberg's oldest houses. The top two stories of the NeuHouse ensemble, which comprises apartments and retail units, are set back, thereby creating space for large terraces with a view of the plaza around the Blumenhalle and the Jewish Museum by Daniel Libeskind. The facades are structured by loggias offset at regular intervals on each floor, while light-colored brick, wood and exposed concrete speak of quality and sophistication. In the constellation with the adjacent historical building, a quiet residential courtyard was created, with private terraces and landscaped communal areas as a place of retreat. The dynamic curves of the corners of the building and its main entrance call to mind another famous Mendelsohn: Erich Mendelsohn's revolutionary Mosse Palais is only a stone's throw from the NeuHouse, in Berlin's newspaper district.

Meatpacking District

Combining the old with the new was also central to the redevelopment of the former slaughterhouses—once the largest and most modern in Europe—on Landsberger Allee in the east of Berlin. Modeled on

New York's Meatpacking District, the new office building, named DSTRCT >170 (pronounced "District"), stands for a new world of work.
The three listed brick halls, which are complemented by buildings in between, offer space for cafés, bars, gyms and shops. The new building, by contrast, offers light-flooded workspaces behind a glass facade that provides a calm backdrop to the red-brick halls. Tall loggias and wide bay windows lend the building rhythm. The loft offices, as co-working spaces, are enhanced by three courtyards and roof terraces with plantings, which create green oases for the tenants from the creative, technology and start-up scene.

A fresh take on the perimeter block

As an exploration of the perimeter block in the history of Berlin's urban development, the building on Franklinstrasse >210 in Charlottenburg demonstrates the free manner in which Gewers Pudewill approach this emotive topic. A new tower, with a metal and glass facade and an inviting main entrance, blends harmoniously with its two existing neighbors via its materials and color, and thereby closes the corner of Salzufer and Franklinstrasse with a view of the Landwehrkanal. A roof terrace, lounge and new courtyards complete the ensemble.

In the best location

One of the last vacant lots on Linienstrasse >74, in downtown Berlin-Mitte, offered space for a new building with 25 apartments and an inner courtyard. The facade of spotless white marble combines clear lines with rounded forms. Loggias variously set

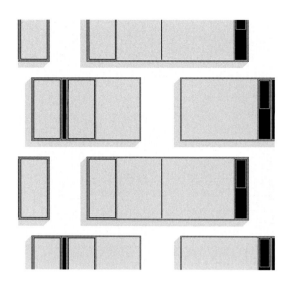

forward and back structure the residential building in Berlin's gallery and art district.

Residential complex on the Stralau peninsula

As part of Berlin's bid to host the 2000 Olympic Games, the Stralau peninsula was earmarked for the Olympic Village. A development company was set up, which planned and went on to construct new buildings, even though the bid ultimately proved unsuccessful. In the mid-1990s, the Rummelsburger Bucht development area was created. Surviving historical industrial buildings, such as the glassworks and the palm oil warehouse, were preserved, and new residential districts were added. On the south bank of the peninsula, opposite Treptower Park, Gewers Pudewill designed a residential quarter in which 75 apartments and town houses are grouped around green courtyards. Large balconies offer views of nature and the water. The apartments are family-friendly and set in a quiet location.

"Colonie-Consens"

The urban villa is a building type that architects and urban planners in Berlin have been reimaging since at least the 1980s and Berlin's International Building Exhibition. In the Prinzenviertel area of Berlin's Karlshorst district, Gewers Pudewill have designed an ensemble that forges a link between the suburban housing estate and the urban villa. The Prinzenviertel was founded in 1893 by the Eigenhaus building association. The Heimstätten-Actien-Gesellschaft purchased the land in order to build a housing colony on a rectangular ground plan with plots of equal size. In 1894, the first Karlshorst houses were constructed. Banking on the local racecourse to attract wealthy buyers, the developers one year later obtained planning consent—the so-called "Colonie-Consens"—for a new estate of "villas and country homes." Many of these historical residences are now listed properties. The ensemble of city villas >110 by Gewers Pudewill takes up key principles of the Gründerzeit era, such as the villa architecture and the emphasis upon green areas. The materials and roof shapes are oriented towards the surrounding houses. The windows, loggias, balconies and sloping reveals, however, are unmistakably modern, as are the staggered story heights. Recessed windows, differently positioned on each floor, lend the facades their plasticity.

White goods

The Technology Center >76 for household appliance manufacturers B/S/H/ Bosch und Siemens Hausgeräte in Spandau combines research departments, offices and technical labs for developing and testing washing machines and dryers. With the goal of making flexibility and the interrelationships between functions easier, Gewers Pudewill designed a clear architecture in which the offices and the laboratories are linked. The building on the Spree consists of a central main body housing the testing facilities and laboratories, to which six office modules are attached. This modular structure and the curves of the metal facades serve to reduce the size of the Technology Center in visual terms. Behind the east facade, which is glazed over six stories, lies the canteen, with an outside terrace directly overlooking the water. The Technology Center represents the transformation of a manufacturing site into a hub of innovation. Saving resources and ensuring energy efficiency are just as essential in the development of today's household appliances as they are in architecture. Thus the heat from the approximately 1,000 washing machines and dryers that are tested here around the clock is used in winter to heat the building. With three acoustics laboratories and a virtual reality laboratory, the Technology Center offers the necessary facilities in which to develop efficient and sustainable washing machines and dryers.

Risky business

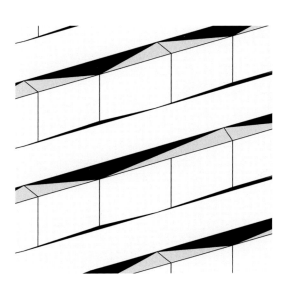

The industrial and commercial buildings on Berlin's Tegeler Weg trace their history back to 1879, when the Schering company built an ether factory here. The building housing Schering's Photographic Department followed six years later, designed by Otto March in the neo-Renaissance style. In 1999, when the company decided to concentrate chiefly on operations at its location in Wedding, only the administrative offices of Schering Deutschland and the technical operations remained in Charlottenburg. The other buildings were leased out, and in 2004 the berlinbiotechpark—Berlin's first biotech and life sciences business park—opened on the site. A particularly striking work of architecture stands at the entrance to the park: the laboratory building by Gewers Pudewill for the German Federal Institute for Risk Assessment >221. While the office workstations are located in the existing building, the new complex is home to the laboratories and their staff. The two premises are connected by a bridge. The laboratory facades exhibit a folded structure, in contrast to the red brick of the older building.

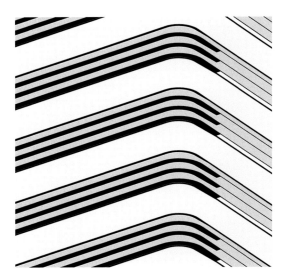

27

"It's not a trick, it's a Sony"

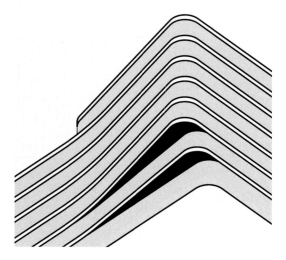

With its music scene and club culture, Berlin has established itself as Germany's music capital. At the European headquarters >64 of the Sony Music Group, Sony Music Publishing and Sony Classical, thousands of artists are looked after: from Roland Kaiser and Bob Dylan to Mark Forster. Following the redevelopment—in a mix of conversion, demolition, renovation and new construction—of the former Commerzbank site in Berlin's Schöneberg district, Sony Music's "Europazentrale" occupies an elegant new building on the corner of Bülowstrasse and Steinmetzstrasse, which once again closes the perimeter block. The area's past links to David Bowie and Iggy Pop fed into Sony Music's decision to relocate from Munich specifically to Schöneberg. For the client, the surroundings and the building signal "independence, urbanity, authenticity and modernity." The offset in the positions of the neighboring buildings was harmoniously resolved by means of an elegant facade movement, visible in the upper stories in rounded facade elements in sophisticated white. The double facade overlooking Bülowstrasse provides acoustic insulation and infuses the building with dynamism. On the Steinmetzstrasse side, the rooftop descends in steps towards the residential buildings, creating room for large roof terraces. Loggias interrupt the facade and give it depth.
The "sound-oriented working landscapes" in the interior were designed by Studio Karhard. The Artist & Repertoire (A&R) departments for Sony Music Entertainment GSA, Sony Music Publishing (Germany) and Sony Classical (Germany), as well as a unit responsible for continental Europe and Africa, are now all under one roof.

"The building symbolizes our aspiration to give the creativity of our artists, employees and partners a magical space," says the Sony company.

Service City

Most Berlin residents and visitors view Berlin Brandenburg Airport—commonly known as BER Airport—as a place of transit. For thousands of people, however, it is also a workplace that shapes their daily lives. This is especially true of four buildings on the airport premises that were designed by Gewers Pudewill. They form part of BER's Service City >68, which comprises the buildings used by the ground-handling and security services, and were intended from the outset to be on an equal architectural footing with the terminal in terms of their design and quality. Through their clear formal language, the exposed concrete buildings convey an impression of "tidiness," as Henry Pudewill says of their design. The administration building for the security services exudes a sense of lightness despite its size, since no supports are visible from the outside. The building is used simultaneously by customs, the Bundespolizei and airport security. In the nearby vehicle hall, the special-purpose vehicles used by the ground-handling services are arranged with optimum efficiency from a logistical point of view. The hall, which is located next to the airport's central workshop, can be flexibly divided and extended. To enable the building to respond to future developments in airport operations, adaptability was a key consideration in its design.

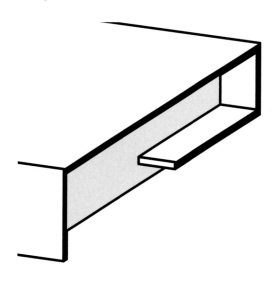

UP!
Berlin-Friedrichshain, Koppenstrasse

Through a radical remodeling, a former GDR department store in Friedrichshain was transformed into a modern workspace for the digital economy.

UP!
Berlin-Friedrichshain, Koppenstrasse

Crystalline incisions break up a cuboid, creating a light-filled, welcoming working environment.

UP!
Berlin-Friedrichshain, Koppenstrasse

Existing buildings with solid structures can find new, contemporary uses,
as demonstrated by the conversion from department store to fluid workspace.

UP!
Berlin-Friedrichshain, Koppenstrasse

Through the addition of three stories, it was possible to compensate for the areas of floor lost due to the incisions in the ground plan. Those working in the building have access to the large roof terrace, which offers unobstructed views over Berlin.

Stream
Berlin-Friedrichshain, Hedwig-Wachenheim-Strasse

The Stream building carries the idea of a new office and working environment for digital natives to new heights, by linking interior and exterior spaces and the floors in ways that have never been seen before in high-rise construction.

Stream
Berlin-Friedrichshain, Hedwig-Wachenheim-Strasse

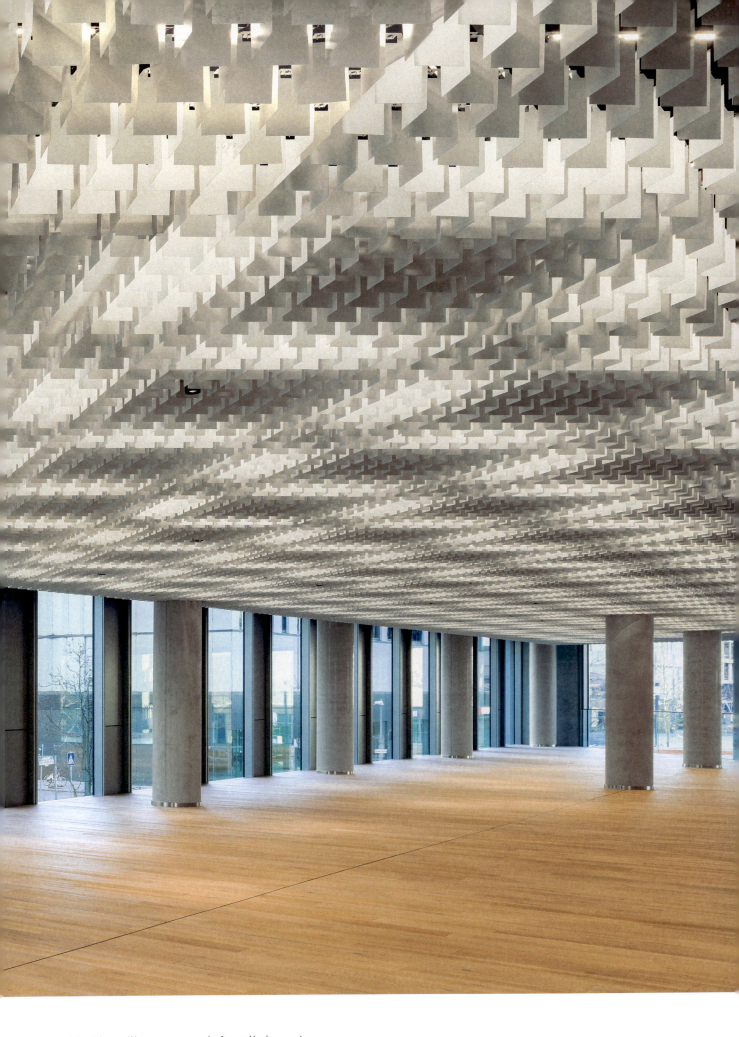

The waffle-like ceiling, composed of small elements, lends the interior space an ethereal and directionless presence.

41

Stream
Berlin-Friedrichshain, Hedwig-Wachenheim-Strasse

Folds and crystalline breaks in the surface lend the building its character.

Stream
Berlin-Friedrichshain, Hedwig-Wachenheim-Strasse

The folded form with its alternately projecting stories gives the tower contours. It is a building without a rear facade. "Beautiful from all sides"—this Renaissance credo is still valid today.

Stream
Berlin-Friedrichshain, Hedwig-Wachenheim-Strasse

As a sculpture in the urban landscape, the 24 stories alternately project and recede like angular folds, allowing spaces for communication and views over the ever-growing city.

Stream
Berlin-Friedrichshain, Hedwig-Wachenheim-Strasse

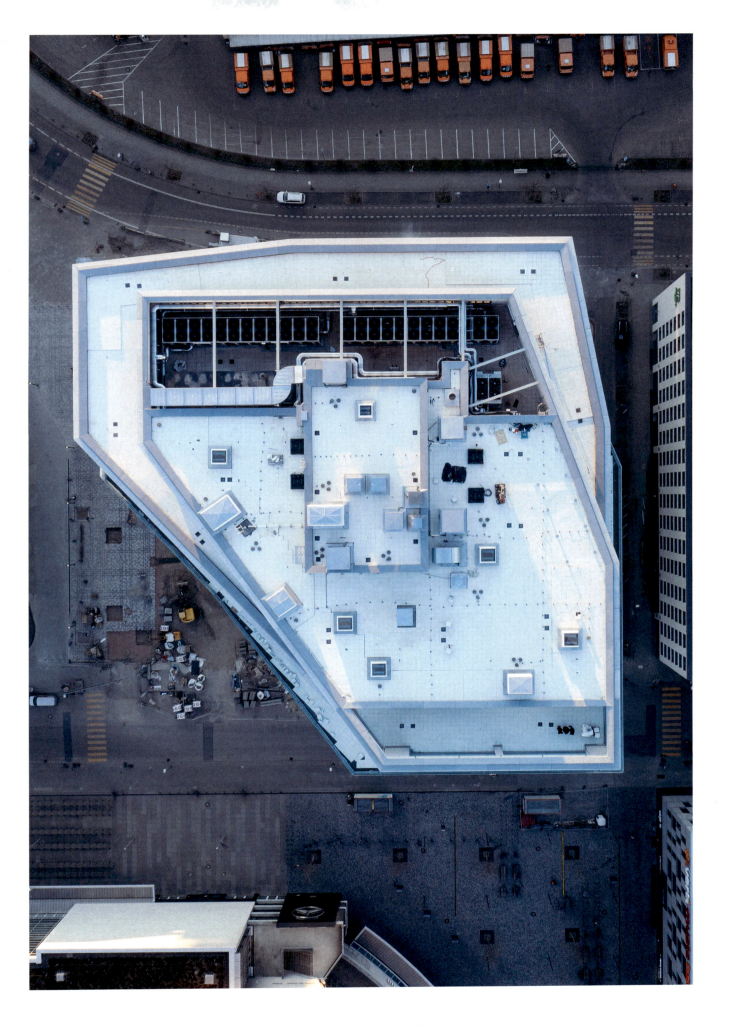

By means of a play with surfaces and volumes, open-air areas are created in
the vertical stories that reference horizontal, ground-level city life.

Stream
Berlin-Friedrichshain, Hedwig-Wachenheim-Strasse

The floor-to-ceiling, large-format glazing ensures a close connection with the city and a fluid transition between inside and outside.

51

Stream
Berlin-Friedrichshain, Hedwig-Wachenheim-Strasse

All workstations and conference rooms enjoy sweeping views of the city and its River Spree—the "Stream."

53

NeuHouse
Berlin-Kreuzberg, Enckestrasse

Not the slightest sense remains here of the history and quality of one of the oldest houses in this part of Berlin. Restoring the building to renewed radiance was a lengthy process.

NeuHouse
Berlin-Kreuzberg, Enckestrasse

The ensemble of old and new overlooks a harmoniously dimensioned plaza around the Blumenhalle and the Jewish Museum by Daniel Libeskind.

NeuHouse
Berlin-Kreuzberg, Enckestrasse

With its curved form, the NeuHouse fits into an area of Berlin that as a whole has seen a turbulent few decades—from the Jewish Museum and the Springer publishing house to the GDR-era tower blocks on Leipziger Strasse.

NeuHouse
Berlin-Kreuzberg, Enckestrasse

With its light clinker-brick facade and elegant curves, the ensemble occupies the plaza in an
agreeable, human scale, and thus also makes the newly created quarter a welcoming place to be.

Im Wirtschaftswunder
Berlin-Schöneberg, Potsdamer Strasse / Bülowstrasse

Leaving the past legible, adding new elements and so upholding the diversity of a lively city—that was the goal directly opposite Bruno Möhring's underground station.

European headquarters of the Sony Music Group
Berlin-Schöneberg, Bülowstrasse

The European headquarters of the Sony Music Group today reside in an elegant new building on the corner of Bülowstrasse and Steinmetzstrasse, which once again closes the perimeter block.

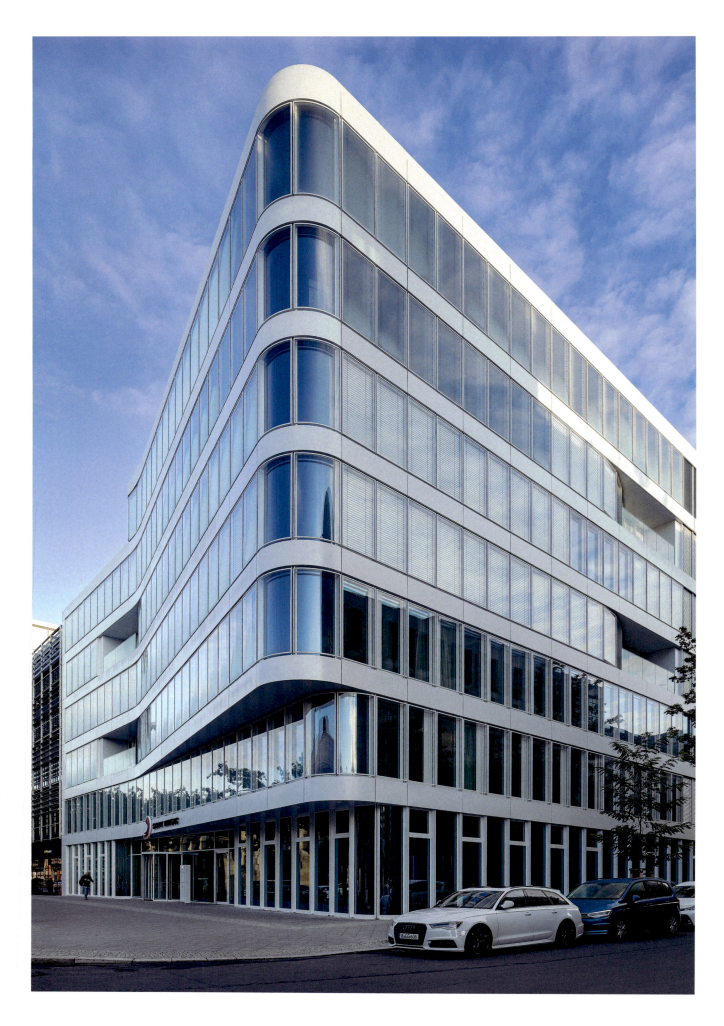

European headquarters of the Sony Music Group
Berlin-Schöneberg, Bülowstrasse

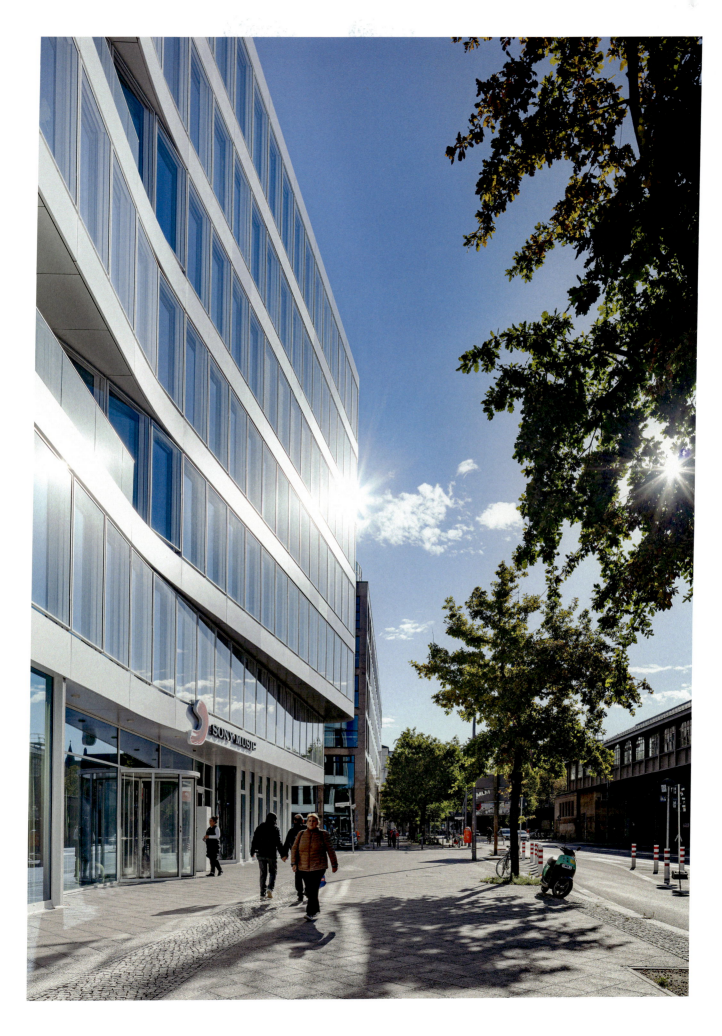

The double facade on Bülowstrasse, which serves as sound insulation, lends the building its very distinctive effect within the urban space.

Berlin Brandenburg Airport Willy Brandt, service buildings
Schönefeld, Service City South

High-quality architecture does not stop at BER's terminal. Ancillary buildings at airports often suffer from a lack of attention to their design— that is not the case here.

Berlin Brandenburg Airport Willy Brandt, service buildings
Schönefeld, Service City South

Despite their different functions and contents, the buildings have a fundamentally kindred character. Seen together, they convey a sense of strength and calm.

Berlin Brandenburg Airport Willy Brandt, service buildings
Schönefeld, Service City South

The design, using large and clear-cut exposed precast concrete elements, expresses timelessness and durability.

Apartment building
Berlin-Mitte, Linienstrasse

The facade of spotless white marble combines clear lines with rounded forms.

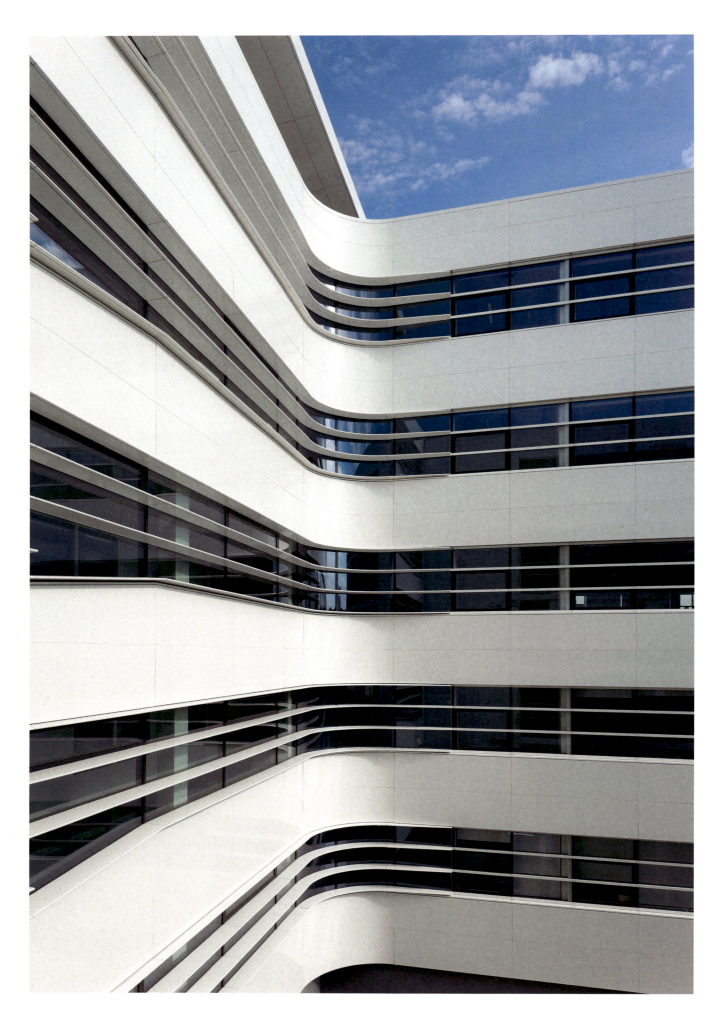
B/S/H/ Bosch und Siemens Hausgeräte Technology Center
Berlin-Spandau, Siemens Technopark

The size of the Technology Center is translated into a human scale by its modular structure and by the curves traced by the metal facades and the wood paneling in the foyer.

B/S/H/ Bosch und Siemens Hausgeräte Technology Center
Berlin-Spandau, Siemens Technopark

The building's idyllic location overlooking the water is an inspiring setting for R&D activities and enhances its architectural effect.

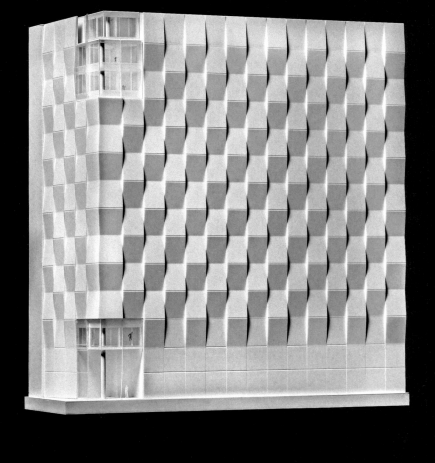

Mercedes-Benz Sales Organization Germany
Berlin-Friedrichshain, Mühlenstrasse

Just as the Mercedes-Benz star on top of the Europa-Center was a landmark of West Berlin in the years before reunification, the company's circular symbol now shines above the new quarter directly behind the Berlin Wall in former East Berlin.

Mercedes-Benz Sales Organization Germany
Berlin-Friedrichshain, Mühlenstrasse

The folded facade cites the undulating waters of the adjacent River Spree and forges a link with the precision of the automotive industry.

Mercedes-Benz Sales Organization Germany
Berlin-Friedrichshain, Mühlenstrasse

The undulating movement of the high-rise's facade is accentuated with pilaster strips on the three accompanying blocks.

Mercedes-Benz Sales Organization Germany
Berlin-Friedrichshain, Mühlenstrasse

The building displays its sculptural effect in the evening sun.

A society that gives everyone access to all aspects of life.

GOAL OF THE LEBENSHILFE E.V.

Spaces for People

If what Winston Churchill said in 1943 is true—"We shape our buildings, and afterwards our buildings shape us"— the social value of architecture is all-important. As the most inescapable art form, architecture is the framework in which our lives unfold every single day, whether at work or at home. In their design of a new residential quarter in Berlin's Köpenick district, for example, Gewers Pudewill have devoted themselves to architecture's most traditional role of all: that of providing a space for living.

Individuality and community—the Joachimstrasse/Lindenstrasse residential park

The fact that perimeter block development does not have to be drab, but can simultaneously foster independence and togetherness through green courtyards and the creation of visual axes, is demonstrated by Gewers Pudewill's proposal for the Joachimstrasse/Lindenstrasse housing project `>116` in Berlin. On behalf of a housing association, the architects designed seven four- and five-story buildings containing a total of 203 subsidized apartments. Since the site is relatively large, courtyards with vegetation, balconies and sight lines form their own, independent spaces. The play of the exterior window frames, which vary in color and shape, reinforces this differentiation. The buildings lying in the interior of the site are oriented towards the south. Inspired by the waves caused by a pebble falling into water, the apartment blocks lead outwards from the interior like widening ripples. A community center offers space for celebrations. More than half of the apartments are low-barrier one- and two-bedroom units. In collaboration with two social agencies, apartments for young people and people living with MS have been integrated into the residential complex. In the L-shaped building wrapping around the Joachimstrasse/Lindenstrasse intersection, four floors at the corner end are used as commercial premises. A day nursery occupies part of the first and second floors. The children have access to a terrace and a playground on the garden side. For a comparatively low budget, Gewers Pudewill have created high-quality living spaces in Köpenick. The residential quarter was a pioneering project by the degewo social housing provider, which after a ten-year hiatus had resumed the construction of new affordable housing.

Mother Courage—"Regine Hildebrandt" Senior Center in Bernau

The "Regine Hildebrandt" Senior Center `>96` stands in landscaped grounds with mature trees and a pond. The building is shaped to fit elegantly into the slightly sunken terrain. The center offers residential apartments for independent living, as well as day care and short-term and full-time nursing care. Large windows allow residents to enjoy fine views of the gardens, including from a chair or a bed. Sliding wooden shutters provide protection from the sun and allow the amount of incoming light to be easily controlled.

Differently positioned depending on use, they animate the clearly structured facade with their variety. Inside the center, color, lighting and materials in warm hues combine to create a pleasantly homely atmosphere and serve as a means of orientation for residents.

The center is named after Regine Hildebrandt, an SPD (Socialist Party of Germany) politician, who was elected to the Volkskammer parliament in the GDR's first free elections. In 1990, she became Minister of Labor and Social Affairs in the first Brandenburg state government, and was elected to the SPD's national executive. Hildebrandt was popular for her open and down-to-earth personality, earning herself the nickname "Mother Courage." In 1991, she was voted Germany's Woman of the Year. This openness is also the inspiration behind the architecture of the senior center named after her.

Swallow nests—Andreashöfe in Berlin

Urban infill can create new, high-quality living spaces—as demonstrated by the construction of the Andreashöfe >120 residential ensemble on an area of land set back behind other buildings in Berlin's Friedrichshain district. The Andreashöfe complex offers 58 quiet, bright apartments around a green courtyard. The main building directly adjoins the seven-story firewall of the neighboring house and has large, deep balconies—not unlike swallow nests—facing south towards the midday sun. The two other architectural elements of the complex are lower in height, and together with the main building form a U-shaped courtyard enclosed on three sides.

The clinker-brick facades of the lower stories are reminiscent of the mews that once stood on this site, and give the houses a timeless quality. This is remarkable in view of the history of their street: the Andreasstrasse was widely known for the opposite of high-grade living. The Gründerzeit neighborhood with its cramped backyards was synonymous with crime and prostitution. Heinrich Zille, who as a child lived in a basement apartment on Andreasstrasse, captured this "Milljöh" in his illustrations and texts. The street suffered extensive damage in the war, and the apartment blocks and two high-rise buildings lining it today were erected in the 1970s. The design by Gewers Pudewill shows how higher density and top-quality spaces can once again be achieved within streets marked by war and socialism.

Secluded and open—Treskowallee residence

The villa on Treskowallee >112 in Berlin's Karlshorst district is located on a piece of land set back behind the houses lining Treskowallee itself. The design establishes an interplay between the two poles of openness and privacy. For while large windows allow a view of the surrounding greenery from inside the rooms, the roof terrace on the top floor is out of sight of the neighbors and offers a quiet place to relax. The first floor consists of a large, flowing space, whose flooring visually links the interior of the villa with the outside terrace. The rooms wrap in a U-shape around three sides of a sheltered courtyard. Elegant white plaster surfaces, on which the leaves of the surrounding trees create a captivating play of shadows in the sunlight, dominate inside and out.

Mercedes-Benz Sales Organization Germany
Berlin-Friedrichshain, Mühlenstrasse

Employees and visitors, as well as the tower and its accompanying blocks, all meet and converge in the lobby.

"Regine Hildebrandt" Senior Center
Bernau, Alte Lohmühlenstrasse

The new building for the Senior Center runs gently along the stands of mature trees towards the far end of the site, and protectively encloses the new oasis of southwest-facing landscaped grounds.

"Regine Hildebrandt" Senior Center
Bernau, Alte Lohmühlenstrasse

The new building winds its way delicately through the mature grounds.

Marquard & Bahls
Hamburg-HafenCity, Koreastrasse

The Hanseatic cog—the emblem of Marquard & Bahls—is carefully implanted in a sandblasted glass wall-structure in the foyer. The wall protects the privacy of the people in the restaurant beyond, but allows a sense of a thriving company.

Marquard & Bahls
Hamburg-HafenCity, Koreastrasse

A double-turn steel staircase, prefabricated in a Hamburg shipyard, forms a focal point in the foyer.

Marquard & Bahls
Hamburg-HafenCity, Koreastrasse

With its special seating, the loggia is an attractive place to spend time even in Hanseatic weather conditions. The directly adjacent café is likewise part of its appeal.

NeuHouse
Berlin-Kreuzberg, Enckestrasse

The facades are structured by loggias offset at regular intervals on each floor, while light-colored brick lends the building a high-quality finish and a fresh lightness.

Residential complex near Tempelhof Airport
Berlin-Tempelhof, Columbiadamm

The light-colored clinker brick makes reference to the facades of Tempelhof Airport opposite.
Material, color and roofline height are oriented towards the famous terminal by Ernst Sagebiel.

Prinzenviertel
Berlin-Karlshorst, Lehndorffstrasse

In Karlshorst's Prinzenviertel district, Gewers Pudewill have designed an ensemble that forges a link between the suburban housing estate by architect Hermann Muthesius and the modern interpretation of a garden-city villa.

Residence
Berlin-Karlshorst, Treskowallee

Operating between the two poles of openness and privacy, the design plays with the possibilities of reusing and infilling a typical Berlin backyard area.

Apartment building
Berlin-Mitte, Linienstrasse

Large areas of glass in the facade elegantly project and recede, giving the building its characteristic structure.

Residential quarter
Berlin-Köpenick, Joachimstrasse/Lindenstrasse

Subsidized housing in the tradition of Max and Bruno Taut, which plays only with formats, color and the penetration of volumes.

Residential quarter
Berlin-Köpenick, Joachimstrasse / Lindenstrasse

Eleven residential buildings follow a guiding architectural theme while varying in their details, creating positive living spaces. The design offers high-quality living at affordable rents.

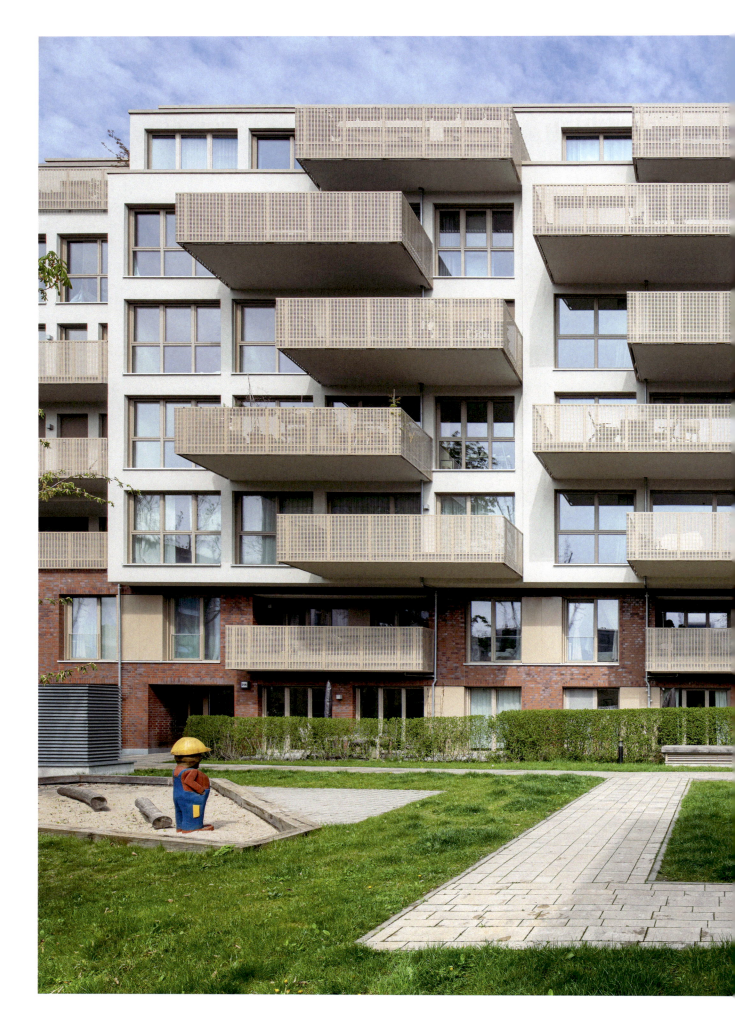

Andreashöfe
Berlin-Friedrichshain, Andreasstrasse

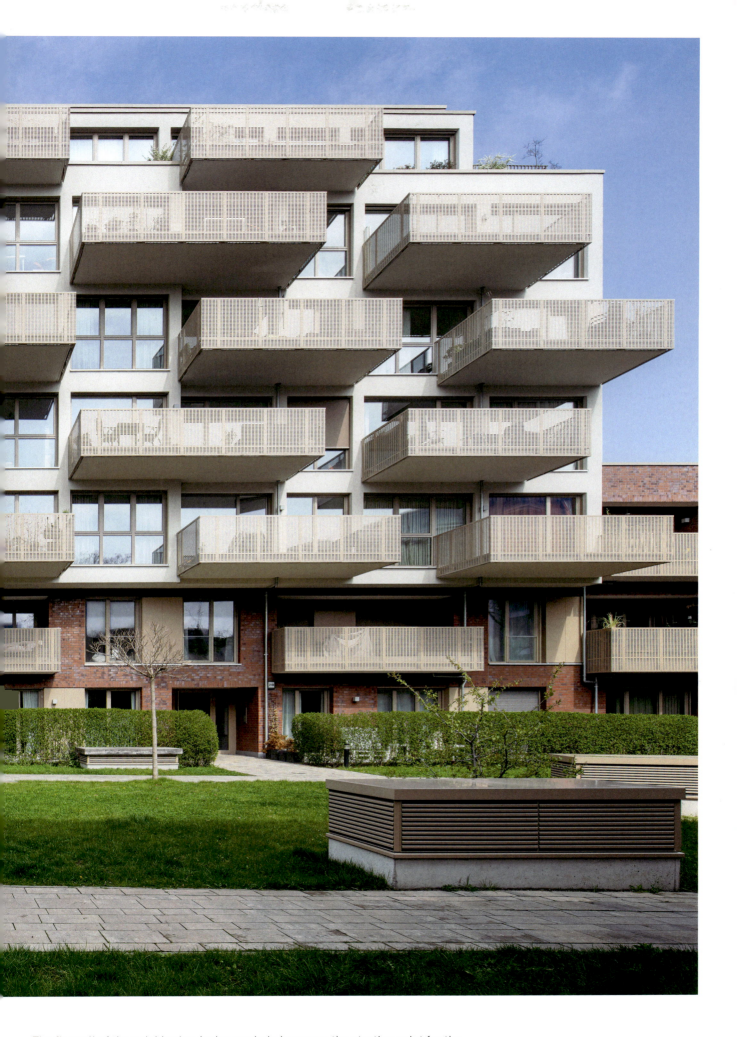
The firewall of the neighboring Andreasschule becomes the starting point for the design of the housing development. The "swallow nests" face south.

121

Andreashöfe
Berlin-Friedrichshain, Andreasstrasse

The couryard development cites the mews that formerly stood on the site, thus establishing an architectural reference to the history of the site.

Villa
Potsdam

On the leafy outskirts of the city, and with a view of Gross Glienicker See lake and the woods, the building has been structured on its narrow dream plot in a surprisingly elegant way by the architects.

DSTRCT
Berlin-Prenzlauer Berg, Landsberger Allee

Bicycle parking on a grand scale: today's mobility transition creates demands that improve life in the city.

DSTRCT
Berlin-Prenzlauer Berg, Landsberger Allee

Carefully transforming the industrial past into today's digital and fluid world of work—that, too, is sustainability.

DSTRCT
Berlin-Prenzlauer Berg, Landsberger Allee

By rejuvenating the interior courtyards, terraces with vertical and horizontal plantings are created on several levels, contributing to a healthier microclimate.

DSTRCT
Berlin-Prenzlauer Berg, Landsberger Allee

The small, interior oases are planted with special ferns, greenery and flowers. They are accessed via wide floor-to-ceiling sliding doors, permitting a fluid transition between inside and outside.

133

Volkswagen Head Office Building
Wolfsburg

The great transparency of the space, combined with a filigree supporting structure, dissolves the boundary between outdoors and indoors, and offers an open and inviting entrance to the office building.

REWAG
Regensburg, Greflingerstrasse

The triangular complex is designed around an inner courtyard. With its varyingly tall and curved longitudinal sides, it responds sensitively to its neighborhood.

independent-

solid—individual

MOTTO OF THE GLOBAL COMPANY MARQUARD & BAHLS AG

Context

On the Silo peninsula—
CentoNew in Rostock

Centogene AG is a leader in the field of genetic tests for the diagnosis of rare diseases. Originally founded as an offshoot of Rostock University, the company's growth resulted in the need for new premises. Its CentoNew >188 building was constructed in an attractive waterfront location on Rostock's Silo peninsula, on the site of a former shipyard. Composed of variously tiered structures, it rises in four stories above an irregular pentagonal ground plan. Above the first floor is a podium, reached by external staircases. Staff and visitors enter a semi-public green atrium that looks out onto the water at both ends. The two structures continuing above it are also oriented so that every employee has a view of the water. The building concludes on the fourth floor in an X-shaped element, which creates space for terraces overlooking the water and makes visual reference to the slipways of the former shipyards. Above a dark clinker-brick base, the finely structured metal-clad facade in warm copper tones wraps itself around the building like a skin.

1950s aesthetic—Volkswagen Head
Office Building in Wolfsburg

Completed in 1959, the Head Office Building >152 of the Volkswagen brand and Volkswagen AG is a Wolfsburg landmark. To enable it to meet the needs of a modern corporate head office, in 2016 the listed building was comprehensively renovated. Restoring the structural fabric was just as important as conserving the subtle, understated 1950s aesthetic. In order to repair and rehabilitate the concrete skeleton, the entire facade had to be removed and subsequently rebuilt. In all, 1,200 windows were replaced, and the systems responsible for fire protection, heating, cooling and data transfer were updated to the latest standards. The office landscape, with its contemporary, high-quality furnishings, makes working for the global group even more attractive. An impressive showroom was also created, providing a setting for presentations of the latest models from Volkswagen AG's many brands. The entrance pavilions with their cantilevered roofs lend the building ensemble an elegant note, and blend in a respectful manner with the company's visual presence on Wolfsburg's Mittelland canal. The fundamental principle

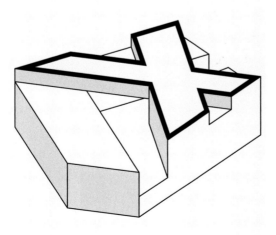

behind their design was to complement a fine work of architecture from Germany's Wirtschaftswunder years with a likewise understated, timeless and elegant extension, one that "respects the past and welcomes the future," as the architects put it.
The administrative building goes back to a pre-war design that was exhibited in Berlin in 1938. The 80-meter-high tower takes up the clinker-brick facade of the long front of the factory, which runs parallel to the Mittelland canal and faces the city. In 1959, when the plant was expanded, the building previously standing on this site was demolished. The current building has been listed since 1989.
Starting in 2013, the office tower was gutted and renovated for energy efficiency. The new two-story-high showroom was created by removing part of the first floor ceiling. The main entrance was moved to the east side.

High-performance ceramics and materials diagnostics—Fraunhofer IKTS

The Fraunhofer Institute for Ceramic Technologies and Systems (IKTS) pursues research and development in the field of high-performance ceramics and materials diagnostics. It is today based in two locations in Dresden and one in Hermsdorf (Thuringia) >164. Together the three sites form Europe's largest research institute for ceramic systems solutions.
Thuringia has a long history of ceramic handcraft and industry. At its Hermsdorf site, Fraunhofer IKTS develops ceramic elements and manufacturing technologies. In order to project these activities to the outside world, the facade consists of fine-grained horizontal bands of light ceramic material. The bands are narrower or wider depending on the use of the space behind them. The facade wraps around the building, which is designed as a parallelogram, and lends the Institute its dynamic face. To preserve this clean silhouette, the building's services and utilities were accommodated in a sunken interior courtyard below the roofline.

REWAG
Regensburg, Greflingerstrasse

Autumnal weather in Bavaria makes the building look like a freestanding solitaire.

REWAG
Regensburg, Greflingerstrasse

Discreet urban renewal within sight of the cathedral in Regensburg's
Old Town, a UNESCO World Heritage Site—what a challenge!

147

REWAG
Regensburg, Greflingerstrasse

Each side of the building responds sensitively to its surroundings in its number of stories, and adapts itself thoughtfully to its neighborhood.

REWAG
Regensburg, Greflingerstrasse

The dynamic and elegant curvatures of the facades soften
the weight and size of the standalone building.

Volkswagen Head Office Building
Wolfsburg

The precisely calculated design of the cantilevered roof is a metaphor for the precision of clearances in the automotive industry, and plays with the image of the uncoated bodywork of a sports car.

Volkswagen Head Office Building
Wolfsburg

The main entrance was moved to the east side.

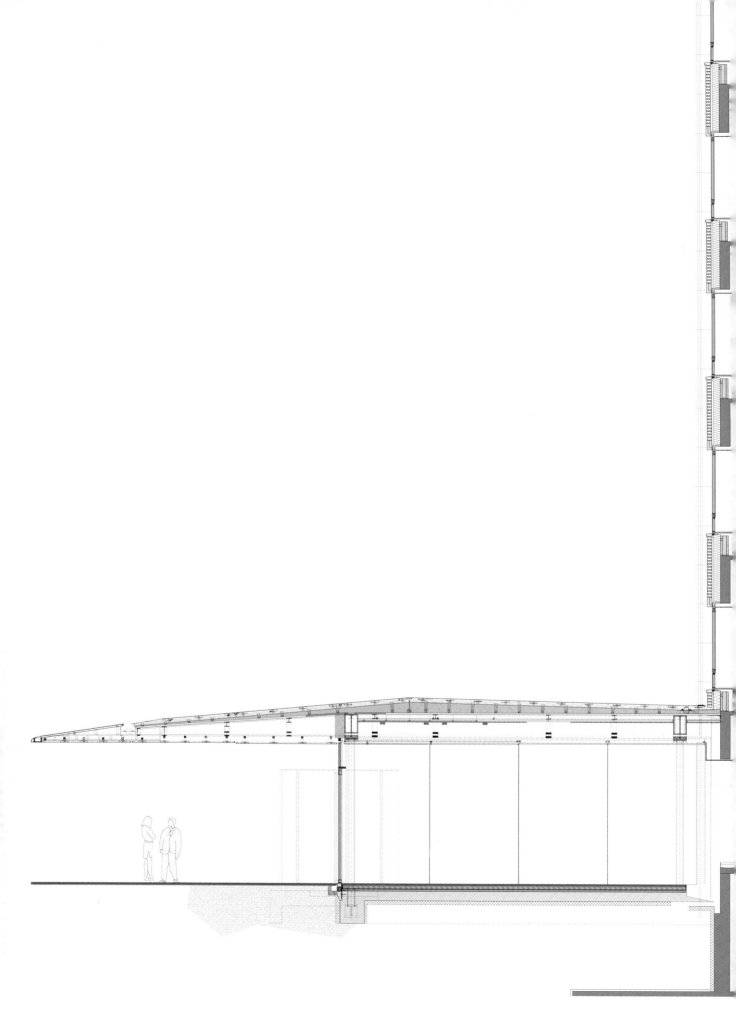

Volkswagen Head Office Building
Wolfsburg

The maximum possible in the simplest beauty.

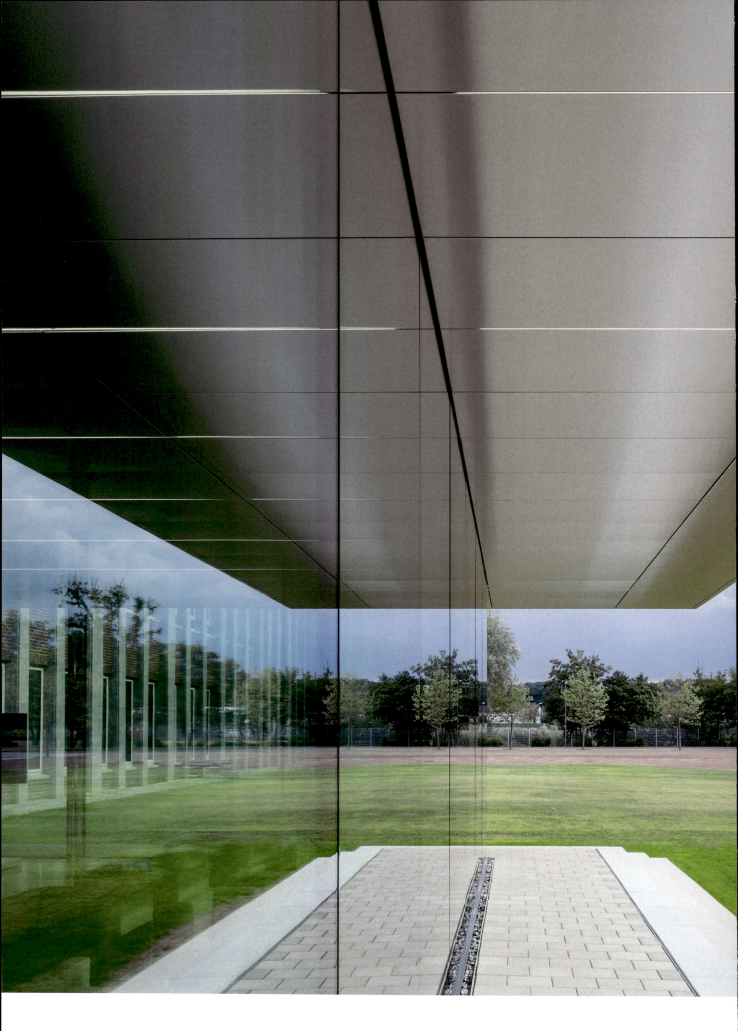

Volkswagen Head Office Building
Wolfsburg

Outside and inside flow into each other and lend the site poetry.

Marquard & Bahls
Hamburg-HafenCity, Koreastrasse

The headquarters of Marquard & Bahls AG are centrally located on Koreastrasse, between the Ericusbrücke and Shanghai-Brücke bridges, in Hamburg's HafenCity district. The very address is an assurance of Hanseatic entrepreneurial spirit.

Marquard & Bahls
Hamburg-HafenCity, Koreastrasse

The building fits confidently into the urban fabric of downtown HafenCity and fills one of the last voids.

Fraunhofer IKTS
Hermsdorf (Thuringia), Michael-Faraday-Strasse

A surrounding area developed in disorderly fashion called for a cohesive design response. It consists of an acute-angled parallelogram, within which the various areas of use interlock like puzzle pieces. The ceramic facade is a discreet reference to the focus of the Institute's research.

Fraunhofer IKTS
Hermsdorf (Thuringia), Michael-Faraday-Strasse

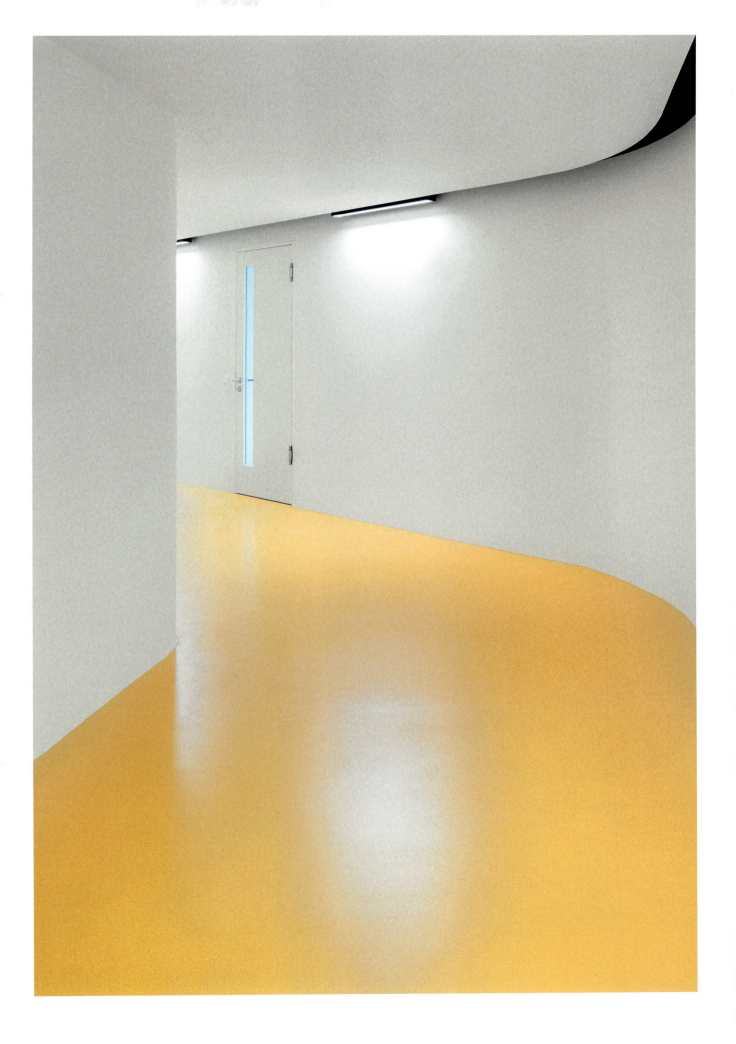

The central access corridor winds through the building like a river.

Residential complex near Tempelhof Airport
Berlin-Tempelhof, Columbiadamm

The two-storied undercut offers a visual axis to the Columbiahalle and lends the building a dramatic sculptural air.

DSTRCT
Berlin-Prenzlauer Berg, Landsberger Allee

Elegant loggias and bay windows run in an undulating movement across
the facade, enabling us to experience the building at the human scale.

DSTRCT
Berlin-Prenzlauer Berg, Landsberger Allee

Tall loggias and wide bay windows rhythmically structure the building.

DSTRCT
Berlin-Prenzlauer Berg, Landsberger Allee

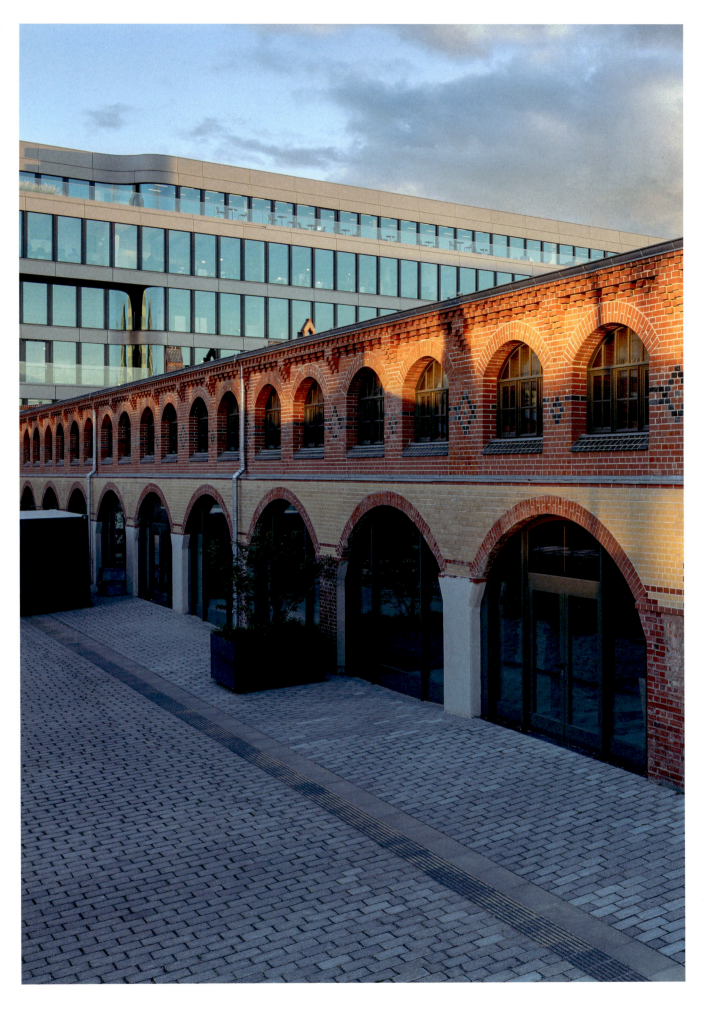

The glass facades of the new building provide a calm backdrop to the clinker-brick halls.
There is no contradiction here between historical and modern.

DSTRCT
Berlin-Prenzlauer Berg, Landsberger Allee

Deindustrialization also means creating new living spaces with new layers: the old beside the new, with a new coding of urban life.

DSTRCT
Berlin-Prenzlauer Berg, Landsberger Allee

The Berlin TV tower beckons in the distance ...

DSTRCT
Berlin-Prenzlauer Berg, Landsberger Allee

The old stands self-confidently next to the new—each with its own legitimacy, each with its own aesthetic. Airy transparency and cool elegance next to historical industrial architecture.

DSTRCT
Berlin-Prenzlauer Berg, Landsberger Allee

Surprising and potent new vistas open up between the centuries.

Fraunhofer IPA
Stuttgart-Vaihingen, Nobelstrasse

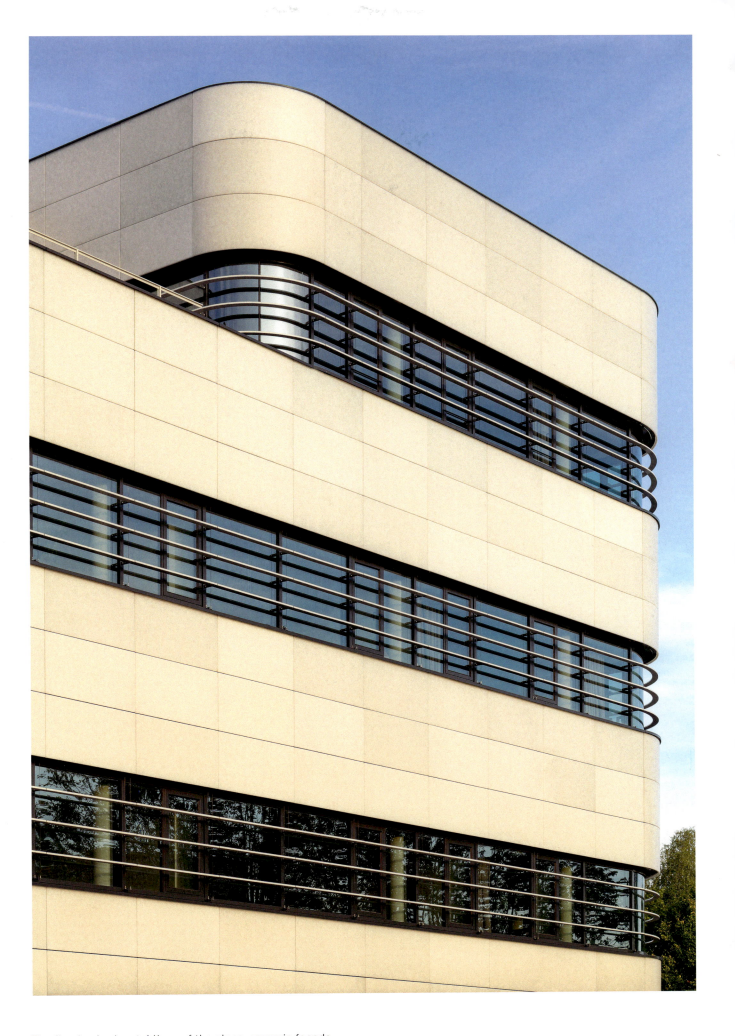
The flowing horizontal lines of the glass-ceramic facade infuse the building with dynamism and lightness.

Fraunhofer IPA
Stuttgart-Vaihingen, Nobelstrasse

The facade, with its glass-ceramic made from recycled glass, lends the building timeless elegance—especially in the evening light.

187

Centogene
Rostock, Am Strande

Leisure and work don't have to exclude each other when it comes to space, but can interact—and in so doing enhance quality of life.

Centogene
Rostock, Am Strande

In its robustness, the sculptural building calls to mind the site's former use as a shipyard, and through its rich complexity ensures an ever-present connection with the water.

Centogene
Rostock, Am Strande

Close to St. Peter's Church and the spot on which Rostock was founded,
CentoNew forms a building block for the old Hanseatic city's future.

Centogene
Rostock, Am Strande

Above the first floor is a podium, reached by external staircases. Employees and visitors enter a semi-public green atrium that opens out onto the water at both ends.

Buildings, in a similar fashion to mechanical watches, have to accommodate all the functions and interconnect them in the best possible way. And must then be provided with a shell that inspires people.

HENRY PUDEWILL

The facade is the face of a building. The design of facades plays a prominent role in the work of Gewers Pudewill, not only because such designs need to fulfill key technical requirements, but also because they are able to produce a sculptural effect. Ever since modernism and its preference for solitaires, buildings have usually had more than one main elevation. In certain cases, the overall planning of the facades can even extend to the roof, which thus becomes the fifth facade.

High-tech curtain-wall and perforated facades

For Georg Gewers in particular, the influence of 1990s British high-tech architecture led at the start of his career to a preference for lightweight curtain-wall glass facades, as in the case of the VNG building in Leipzig. The aspect of the climatic envelope was thereby more important than the elevation. The elegant details, which require no frame, convey the impression of a support-free glass facade. Curtain-wall facades do not have to carry loads, because in the skeleton construction method these are borne by columns and cores. Part of the canon of modern architecture ever since Walter Gropius's Fagus factory in Alfeld an der Leine, curtain-wall facades can thus become an expression of interior and function.

Wood, natural stone, metal, plaster and clinker brick

In Gewers Pudewill's later work, high-tech glass facades are joined by mineral and perforated facades. Rear-ventilated facades are constructed as a sandwich of cladding, air gap and thermal insulation.

Cascade—The UP! in Berlin

A good example of a sculptural approach to a facade design is the UP! building >206 in Berlin, whereby the cascade-like form is not an artistic end in itself, but serves to bring better lighting and ventilation into the deep floor plans of the existing building. The facades of the former Centrum department store, constructed in 1978, were opened on all sides by means of incisions over the entire height of the building. This intervention creates four spectacular canyons with green terraces and generous glazing, which allow light and air to flow into the offices. The architects have chosen a "subtractive" approach to the conversion. A unique contrast is established between an elegant facade and interiors that have been left "raw." Providing the ground plan with natural light by means of incisions on all four sides led to the distinctive image of terraced facades presented by the UP! building. While the north-facing sides of the canyons descend vertically, all other sides are stepped downwards in a cascade of open terraces. The facade is in part opaque, while the incisions are accented by clear glass elements. On the smooth facades on the outer edge, on either side of the incisions, every fourth field is opaque and has an opening vent. This latter gives employees the means of influencing the lighting and ventilation at their workstations—an important consideration for their well-being. The terraces, with their larch wood flooring, present a warm contrast to the cool green elements of the facade.

Sur/faces

REWAG headquarters in Regensburg

In the case of the new headquarters for REWAG >144 (the Regensburg energy and water supply company) and the Regensburg Stadwerke (municipal utilities), the aim was to create an office and administrative building with contemporary workspaces, in which employees and customers feel welcome and enjoy spending time. The triangular structure is designed around an inner courtyard, and with its curving longitudinal sides of varying heights responds sensitively to its neighborhood. Warm, light-colored materials such as wood in the interior harmonize with the Kehlheim limestone used for the facades. The pale stone cladding has been variously worked so that it reflects the incident light. Traditional stonemasonry techniques, such as the bush-hammering and scarfing of the horizontal stone bands, serve to enhance the effect of the facade in different lighting conditions and angles of incidence.

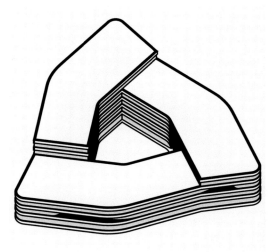

Green rooms—Stream office tower in Berlin

Standing not far from the UP! building, the Stream office tower >234 is an unmissable presence in Berlin's new Mediaspree quarter. Its facade is hallmarked by two materials: floor-to-ceiling glazing and bands of exposed concrete. The tower has no rear side(s), but radiates in all four directions of the compass with its sculptural form. A sophisticated interplay is established between interior and exterior spaces and likewise between selected floors. Alternating projections and recesses, resembling angular folds, lend the high-rise its distinctive form.

The workspaces are located along the facade and are punctuated by "green rooms" and "living rooms," where employees can meet and chat. The wraparound and tapering terraces, as well as the internal seating-cum-staircases each connecting two levels, also serve as places of relaxation and stimulation for the office tower's users. The terraces on each floor run in some cases around two corners and so provide ample space for creative breaks, conversations, innovative ideas and views over Berlin's most exciting new urban district. Neither the undersides of the regularly projecting stories nor the base differentiate themselves in terms of design from the Stream's facades.

The bands of the facade, tracing an angular "S," follow a rhythm that sometimes spans two floors, sometimes just one. The undercut ends in truncated soffits. Only two-thirds of the facade surfaces consist of glass. They are shaded for the most part by the projecting stories above. Ventilation flaps that can be manually opened enable all employees to enjoy fresh air at their desks. This is an important quality for the new office and working environment of today's digital natives. Indirect lighting illuminates the undersides from below, lending the Stream tower a mesmerizing glow in the twilight. The interplay between rough and smooth that characterizes the facade arises from the contrast between exposed concrete and glass.

Room with a view in Potsdam

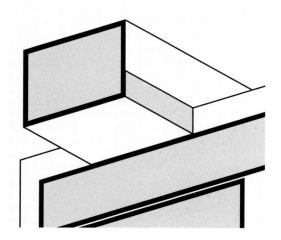

Modernist architecture repeatedly sought to remove from the facade its character of a divider between outside and inside. The design by Gewers Pudewill for the villa in Potsdam >228 adopts a completely different approach. On this narrow dream plot on the leafy outskirts of the city, offering a view of the Gross Glienicker See lake and the woods, the architects have layered different structures one on top of the other. Through its offset elements, this form has the advantage of creating large terraces that link inside and outside not just in visual terms. The large glass facades facing the water can be directly opened up to the natural world outside. The remaining facades are made of Vals gneiss, a dense and highly prized natural stone from the Swiss Alps. The butted, seamless and partially polished surface gives the villa a powerful yet calm facade.

Ceramic gleam—Fraunhofer IKTS in Hermsdorf

When it came to the extension building for the Fraunhofer IKTS >214 at the Hermsdorf freeway intersection, it seemed logical to choose a material for the facade that referenced the research being carried out on-site. The Fraunhofer Institute for Ceramic Technologies and Systems (IKTS) develops ceramic materials and manufacturing technologies for structural and functional ceramics. In order to show the work of the Institute to the outside world, too, the facade is composed of finely articulated horizontal bands of a light-colored ceramic material, which are narrower or wider depending on the use of the space behind them. The facade wraps around the pointed parallelogram like a skin and gives it a gleaming appearance. To avoid any interruption to the clear silhouette, the building's services and utilities are concealed in a sunken interior courtyard below the roofline.

Wave motion—
Im Wirtschaftswunder in Berlin

When the former Commerzbank headquarters on Potsdamer Strasse in Berlin were converted into the Forum >238, as part of the Im Wirtschaftswunder office and retail ensemble, Gewers Pudewill gave the building an elegant new facade. Its interplay between old and new matches the Forum's location on Potsdamer Strasse, whose charm comes from its diversity. The bank building, which formerly presented a closed-off impression, has now received a white, undulating facade.

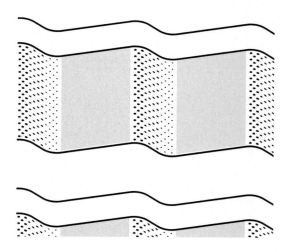

New shell—Carl Zeiss Meditec AG in Berlin

The berlinbiotechpark in Charlottenburg is one of the most important locations for companies in the technology and life sciences sectors. On behalf of Carl Zeiss Meditec AG >222, a production and warehouse building from the 1960s was converted into an office complex with training rooms, offices and communal spaces. As part of this project, the entire shell was renewed. Flowing lines on the facade convey movement and establish the building's aesthetic independence on the campus. A white pattern in an algorithmic gradient was printed on the facade glazing, which on the north side is floor-to-ceiling. The result is a cool light effect, similar in quality to an ice crystal, in keeping with the sterile, medical use of the building.

Fraunhofer IPA in Stuttgart—
Processing Technologies in
Lightweight Construction (BTL)

At the Stuttgart campus of the Fraunhofer Institute for Manufacturing Engineering and Automation (IPA), the new building >230 for the BTL department follows the contours of the street and the geometry of a neighboring plaza, whose steps extend all the way into the lobby. The flowing, horizontal lines of the glass-ceramic facade infuse the building with a sense of dynamism and lightness. Lying behind the facade are modern and bright offices, seminar rooms, laboratories and a hall.

A solid Hanseatic house—
Marquard & Bahls headquarters in Hamburg

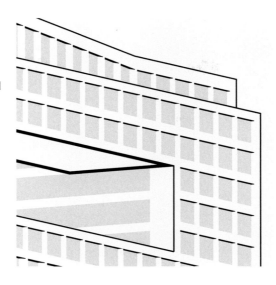

The headquarters >216 of Marquard & Bahls AG were constructed on one of the last vacant lots in Hamburg's HafenCity. The brick building translates the global company's motto into architecture: "independent—solid—individual." Elegant and at the same time robust, it fits harmoniously into its neighborhood and thereby sets its own clear accent. The atrium is linked to the public space by the loggia, a large opening in the facade. Looking through it, all rooms have a view of the water. The building and the company thus open up to the city and the light. The ninth story draws the eye with its offset design, and marks the high and end point of the building overlooking Brooktorhafen harbor basin.

Centogene
Rostock, Am Strande

The calm and vibrancy of a walk-through sculpture.

NeuHouse
Berlin-Kreuzberg, Enckestrasse

The building's sculptural approach is reinforced by the understated entrances with their elegant, inviting gesture.

UP!
Berlin-Friedrichshain, Koppenstrasse

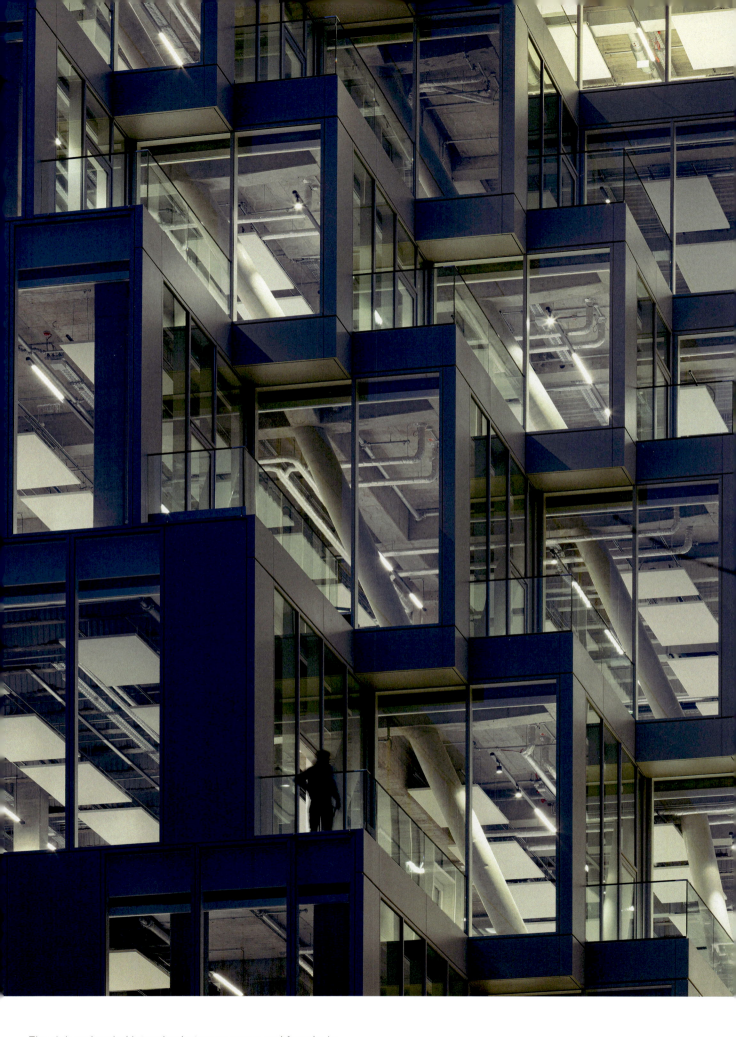

The rich and varied interplay between space and facade, in conjunction with precision in the details, offers ever new perspectives.

UP!
Berlin-Friedrichshain, Koppenstrasse

Terrace spaces at the human scale became an architectural motif.

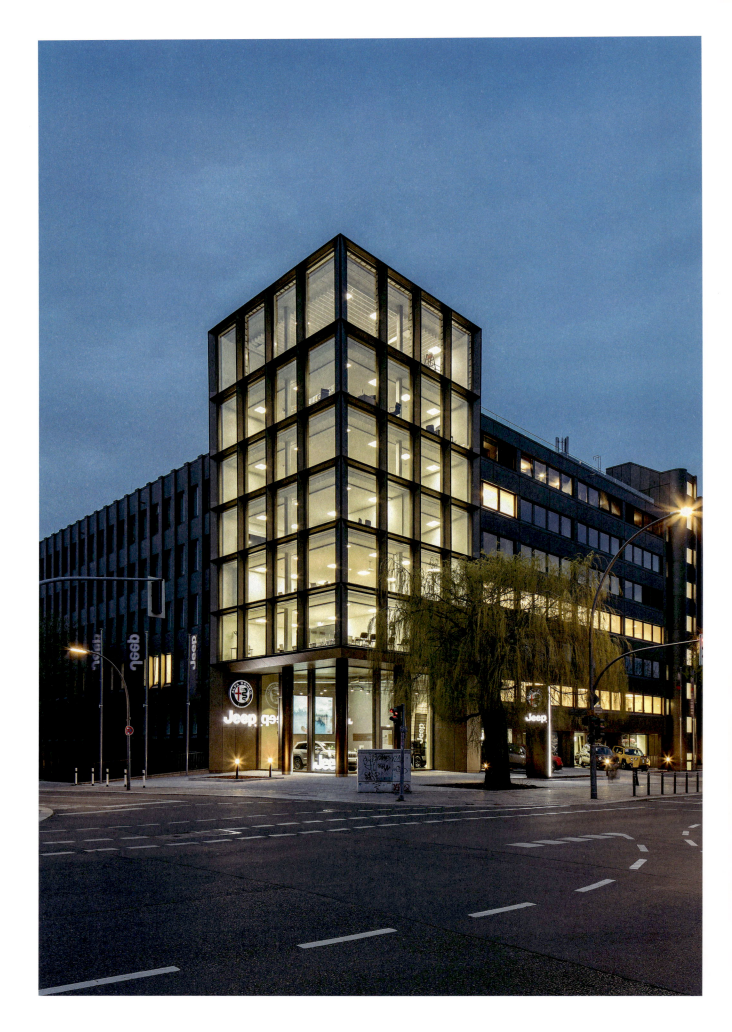

Bürohaus
Berlin-Moabit, Franklinstrasse

The transparent corner tower heals a decades-old urban-planning wound and enables traditional building structures to be perceived once again as integral elements of the cityscape.

B/S/H/ Bosch und Siemens Hausgeräte Technology Center
Berlin-Spandau, Siemens Technopark

Working beside the water in light architecture.

Fraunhofer IKTS
Hermsdorf (Thuringia), Michael-Faraday-Strasse

Precision and durability characterize the ceramic facade and the work of the research institute in equal measure.

Marquard & Bahls
Hamburg-HafenCity, Koreastrasse

Hanseatic restraint, enduring value and attention to detail
are the key characteristics of the Marquard & Bahls building.

Marquard & Bahls
Hamburg-HafenCity, Koreastrasse

Double-walled with a double turn, prefabricated in a shipyard, more of a boat's hull than a staircase—you can't get more Hamburg than that.

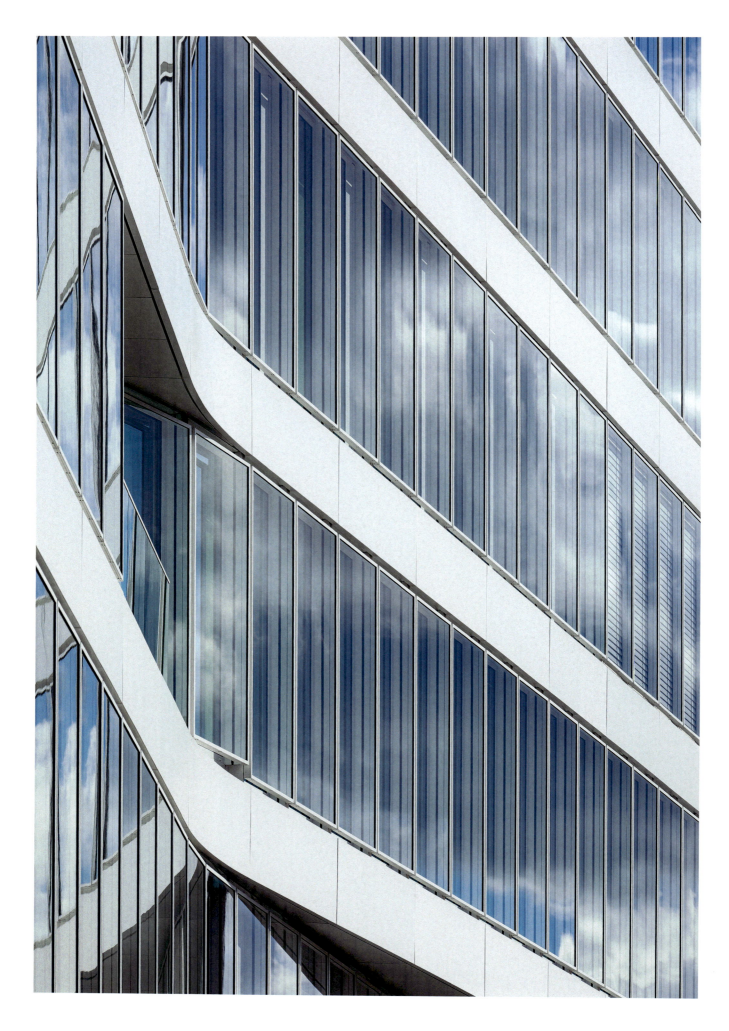

European headquarters of the Sony Music Group
Berlin-Schöneberg, Bülowstrasse

German Federal Institute for Risk Assessment
Berlin-Charlottenburg, Max-Dohrn-Strasse

Carl Zeiss Meditec
Berlin-Charlottenburg, Max-Dohrn-Strasse

The gradient print gives a frosty, clean impression.

Residential complex near Tempelhof Airport
Berlin-Tempelhof, Columbiadamm

Loggias in urban density as a leitmotif of timeless facades.

Apartment building
Berlin-Mitte, Linienstrasse

Precise composition of joins and openings in a facade of Lasa marble.

Villa
Potsdam

Butt joints of millimetric precision and rough surfaces of quarried Vals gneiss reinforce the villa's sculptural effect.

Fraunhofer IPA
Stuttgart-Vaihingen, Nobelstrasse

Horizontal window bands with fins infuse the white structure with dynamism.

Berlin Brandenburg Airport Willy Brandt, service buildings
Schönefeld, Service City South

Airports are about arrival and departure. Speed and movement are themes taken up in the orientation of the facade openings, too.

Stream
Berlin-Friedrichshain, Hedwig-Wachenheim-Strasse

In its raw, archaic functionality, the core as the backbone of the high-rise is reduced to the absolute essentials: traffic and stability.

REWAG, Regensburg
Facade material: Kehlheim limestone

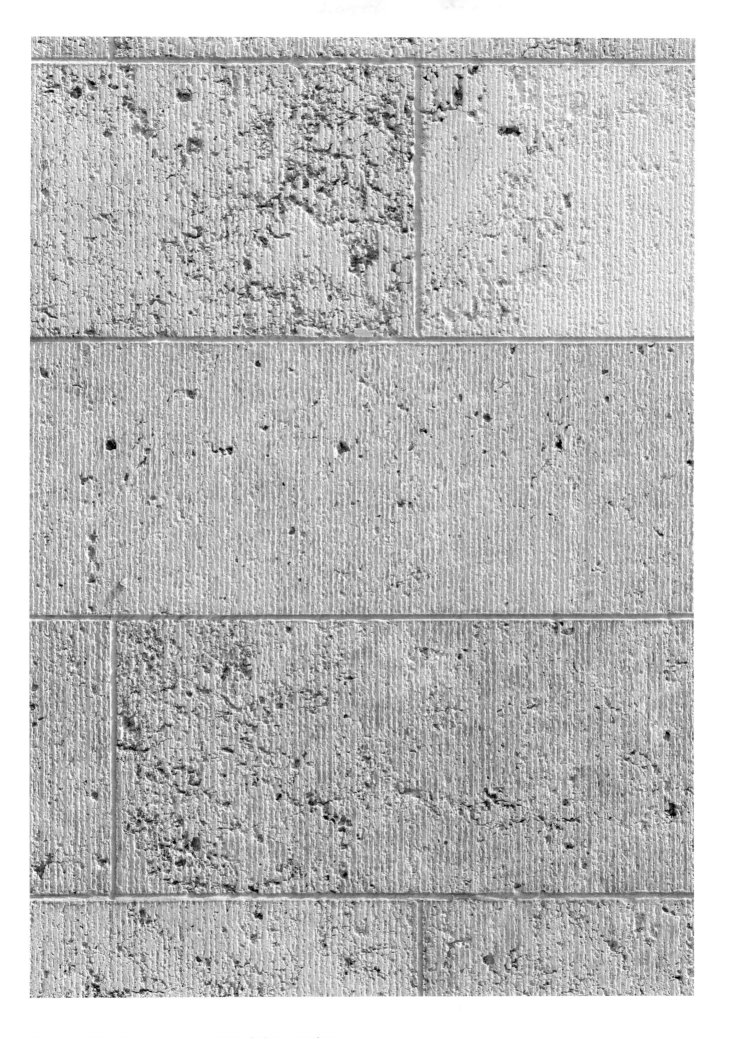

By means of traditional stonemasonry techniques, such as
bush-hammering and scarfing, the stone is given new surfaces.

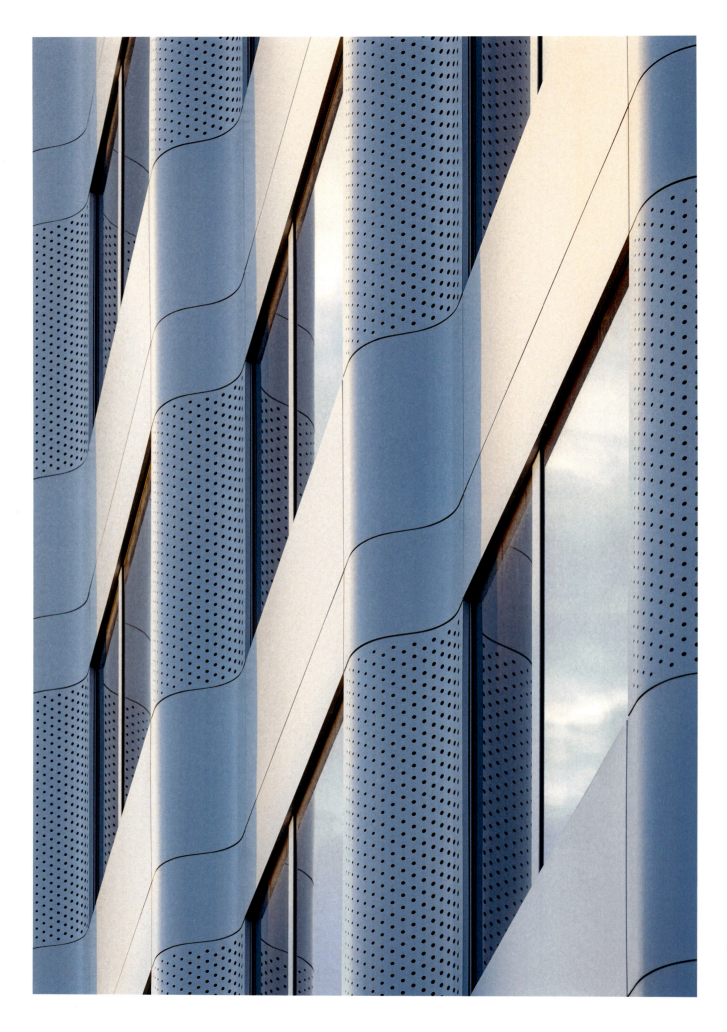

Im Wirtschaftswunder
Berlin-Schöneberg, Potsdamer Strasse/Bülowstrasse

The stately existing staircase was retained and given new surroundings.

Stream
Berlin-Friedrichshain, Hedwig-Wachenheim-Strasse

Surprising and fresh: the elevators in the Stream building provide variety on the way to the workplace.

Mercedes-Benz Sales Organization Germany
Berlin-Friedrichshain, Mühlenstrasse

The subtle play of the folds on the facade is enhanced by a lighting concept in the interstices.

The art of building is sculpture on a grand scale, and architecture one of the few areas that give a city its face.

GEWERS PUDEWILL

Backstage

As architects,
Georg Gewers and
Henry Pudewill
have different
characteristics and
profiles. But when
it comes to designing
relevant buildings,
they are of one mind.

The value of materials

*"It is neither necessary nor possible
to invent a new architecture every
Monday morning."*

LUDWIG MIES VAN DER ROHE

This *bon mot* by the most famous German architect of the twentieth century also describes one of the fundamental views held by Georg Gewers and Henry Pudewill in their work. Instead of losing themselves in pseudo-original contortions, they design precise, aesthetically multifaceted buildings of all different kinds, which are tailored to fit the needs not just of the client, but also of the city, the users, and society in the broadest sense. The two founders and owners of the architectural office of Gewers Pudewill look back on very different early careers, but share the same way of working when designing and a common interest in references. They thereby draw primarily from three sources: organic architecture, the British high-tech architecture of the 1990s and the office-building architecture of early 1930s Berlin.

The works by representatives of organic architecture, such as Alvar Aalto, were a formative influence. Aalto was the protagonist of a different modernism, one that was not rational, cold and repetitive in the manner of construction industry functionalism, but more humane, rounder, friendlier and more fluid. Just as the name Aalto stands at the beginning of every dictionary of architecture, it also stands at the start of Gewers Pudewill's exploration of architecture. The pioneer of modernism in Northern Europe, whose works are situated inside and outside of time, personified the value of materials and sculptural mastery—qualities that also distinguish the work of Gewers Pudewill.

The term "organic architecture" describes not only convex-concave, non-Euclidean geometries and rounded corners in architecture, but also the harmonious relationship of the part to the whole.

Aalto's designs are softer than the rational modernism practiced by Ernst Neufert and other, more dogmatic architects of classical modernism, but are nevertheless of great clarity. His buildings respond more flexibly to their respective location—and are designed right down to the smallest detail, as in the case of the famous bronze door handles that Aalto created for his buildings, and which he mounted one below the other to suit users of different heights. For Aalto, the door handle and handrail were the points at which the human body comes into direct contact with a building—"the handshake of the building," as it has been called. In works such as his Finlandia Hall in Helsinki, Aalto had the stair handrails wrapped in leather, so that they would not feel cold to the touch. Gewers Pudewill, too, strive for an architecture that is simultaneously more sculptural, more personal and more humane—without seeking direct similarities with the Finnish master in their work.

High-tech architecture likewise uses nature as a model, both for broad-span constructions and for more abstract physical observations, as in the case of the double facade. Gewers Pudewill contrast what Karl Bötticher called the core form and the art form with the "performance form."

The high-tech architecture practiced in Britain by architects such as Norman Foster, Nicholas Grimshaw, Michael Hopkins and Richard Rogers was fascinating for all architects of the 1990s. Although high-tech architecture was perceived as a school, it encompassed a vast spectrum of design approaches, ranging from Foster's rigid, austere and indeed exclusive architecture to the delight taken by Rogers in the use of color and playful form.

Georg Gewers gained important experience as a young architect working for Foster Associates in London. Sophisticated and ingenious large-scale projects and transport buildings, such as Stansted Airport, were being designed in Foster's office on the Thames at the time. Gewers learned to design and build with Foster's elegance as part of the team creating the Business Promotion Center in Duisburg.

Looking back to the past

Gewers Pudewill had to argue the case with the Berlin urban-planning authorities for their crystalline-glass design for the headquarters of the Mercedes-Benz Sales Organization >80 in the Mediaspree district. Berlin's building policy was at that time aimed solely at urban repair and oriented towards the "good old days." But "Berlin is different," to cite Gewers Pudewill. To play ugly late modernism off against the city's handsome classicist buildings, or its pre-modern architecture in general, is too simplistic as a line of argument. Berlin had already undergone a profound transformation even between Karl Friedrich Schinkel's era and the Gründerzeit of the 1870s, and proceeded to develop rapidly at the end of the nineteenth century. Then came the 1920s, with the result that every 20 years a fundamentally new architecture took its place in the city, including as a result of war, the Holocaust and the division of Germany. Constantly referencing the history of the old Berlin, in other words, is not always sufficient. In the 1920s in particular, Berlin was a world leader in the field of architecture, and the home and domain of architects of the first order, such as Peter Behrens, Le Corbusier, Ludwig Mies van der Rohe and Erich Mendelsohn.

The second tier includes designers of Berlin's office architecture of the late 1920s and early 1930s—outstanding architects who make the supposed conflict between glass and stone seem absurd in view of the elegance of their buildings, which combine both materials in seemingly effortless fashion. Today these buildings are an excellent point of reference for modern metropolitan architecture that is neither merely modern nor merely retrospective.

Emil Fahrenkamp's Shell-Haus and Bruno Paul's high-rise complex for the Kathreiner company next to Kleistpark are examples of a different modernism that was not represented at the Bauhaus and which blossomed in Berlin outside the canon laid down by Walter Gropius. Happily, Gewers Pudewill's engagement with the architecture of this period is not solely intellectual: they are currently remodeling the Femina Palast designed in 1931 in Berlin by Richard Bielenberg and Josef Moser, and thereby adding a new layer of time to it.

Georg Gewers and Henry Pudewill first met in 1996 in Berlin, while both working in very different Berlin architectural offices, and remained friends over the next ten years. In 2007, since the timing was at that point auspicious, they founded their own office—an "architecture manufactory," as they called it. Thanks to its success, the manufactory did not stay small for long, and Gewers Pudewill soon had over 30 employees. But size is not everything: on the contrary, it remained important to the two owners to be closely involved in their projects, and so be able to engage intensively with the team and the building in question. Gewers Pudewill is distinguished from other offices by its history.

Shell-Haus
Berlin
Emil Fahrenkamp, 1932

Both founders had already built up a wealth of experience and a good reputation, which enabled them to survive the first few years, when the office could still show little in the way of turnover or references. Everything related to the two founders as people. Several positive factors came together, however, to ensure the office's success: the healthy economy, the architects' focus on Berlin, the influx of young people and the fact that Berlin finally developed its own momentum in the noughties. When Berlin boomed, the Gewers Pudewill office was already well positioned to catch the wave. The architects were masters of their craft and had design ideas aplenty.

In the initial years after its foundation, the office designed numerous projects abroad, including in China, Saudi Arabia and Russia. Although these were exciting projects, it proved impossible to turn them into reality. Construction in Germany may be stodgy and slow at times, but when a project goes ahead, it goes ahead. Happily, Gewers Pudewill found clients who believed in the future of Berlin and had exciting commissions to award. They also brought their own dedicated commitment, as a decisive quality, to this series of fortunate coincidences.

First projects

Gewers Pudewill's first client was a home-building company, which in 2009 commissioned an apartment complex in Berlin's Linienstrasse >114. Even in this first building, the bright white facade convincingly showed how clear lines can be combined with rounded forms.

The architects' first major project, however, was for the ancillary buildings at Berlin Brandenburg Airport >68. The contract was awarded in 2008/9 and construction needed to be completed by 2011.

Gewers Pudewill were eager to find out how the airport functions behind the scenes, because "at that point the airport no longer understood what it was," as Henry Pudewill says. Gewers Pudewill therefore began by holding design workshops with the buildings' users. Clients who feel they are being taken seriously are more likely to identify with their construction projects. This was one of the keys to success. The buildings for the ground-handling services, security services, central workshop and main vehicle hall were completed on time and on budget.

But then came the news that the airport would not yet go into operation as planned. It was finally opened without fanfare in 2020. "No one wanted anything more to do with the airport," Gewers Pudewill recall. As a consequence, one of their largest early projects received little media attention.

The commission for the headquarters of the Mercedes-Benz Sales Organization in Berlin's new Mediaspree district, on the other hand, was a decisive milestone, owing to their visibility: the Mercedes-Benz buildings are large and stand at the heart of the new Berlin, in the then still undeveloped

Kathreiner high-rise
Berlin
Bruno Paul, 1930

Mediaspree area. The next major commission came from B/S/H/ Bosch und Siemens Hausgeräte >212. The domestic-appliance company initially wanted to build in the berlinbiotechpark in Charlottenburg, for which Gewers Pudewill drew up the master plan. Ultimately, however, its new Technology Center was constructed in the Siemensstadt district. Given its focus on white goods, B/S/H/ wanted a building that did not look too expensive or too showy. With a few sleights of hand, Gewers Pudewill succeeded in designing an elegant complex. They were thereby aided by their unpretentious, calm and self-confident approach to design.

Tailored to requirements

It is essential to Gewers Pudewill that the partnership between client and architect should be one of respect. Clients who only think about money often don't care about architecture. For Gewers Pudewill, good architecture is only achieved when buildings—for whatever area of life—produce an added value, going beyond the material dimension, for their clients. With each of their designs, Gewers Pudewill first carry out an analysis of needs, conduct structured conversations with clients and users, and listen closely in order to understand what they want. People tend to think they already know what the other person wants, but "we don't have the answer right away" is one of the office's maxims. This analysis of needs at the planning stage reveals the demands the building must fulfill. Gewers Pudewill are concerned with understanding the picture in their client's mind, and with interpreting and supporting the client's ideas in the language of architecture. It is only in personal conversation that many clients open up. Such talks help construct a complete picture of the design and a shared sense of the building project.

The following anecdote illustrates this well. Gewers Pudewill have won many commissions with their needs analyses, including for the extension to the Porsche customer center in Leipzig, which was designed by gmp. These celebrated architects later thanked Gewers Pudewill for treating their building with such care. This restraint should not be confused with blind devotion. Gewers Pudewill had to rethink the whole building and facilitate the "parallelization of processes." Rather than marking out their separate territory, however, they worked intelligently with the existing structure, "because it proved to be robust." The alterations to the customer center are only visible at second glance—something that expresses Gewers Pudewill's attitude. Soon afterwards, another major German carmaker, Volkswagen AG, approached Gewers Pudewill as a client.

IG Metall building
Berlin
Erich Mendelsohn, 1930

"We enjoy developing architecture and like working with people. Our clients sense that."

HENRY PUDEWILL

When a commission grips their imagination, they can't disguise it and enthusiastically start designing. When the urban community later accepts the building, and people say, "That's not the modern architecture we're not usually interested in, but something exciting," that fills the two designers with deep satisfaction. Gewers and Pudewill wish to be seen by their clients not as service providers, but as partners.

Gewers and Pudewill are an architectural duo in a city full of architectural duos. They complement each other in their profiles. One designs more "from the inside," the other more "from the outside"—because architecture is the art form that creates interior spaces while forming exterior spaces, and it can't do one without doing the other. Gewers Pudewill don't like "houses that you wrap in a fancy evening gown, only to have to resort to a sledgehammer when it comes to making them work inside, because things just don't want to fit together," as they put it. Architects can't start by thinking solely from the inside out, because the surrounding urban environment already exists. Inside and outside have to be created at the same time. Gewers Pudewill develop none of their designs without good, functioning processes: it is an iterative procedure. Research complexes and industrial buildings are usually solitaires and located in weaker contexts in terms of urban planning, but apartment buildings and even laboratory facilities such as CentoNew >188 often place their stamp on inner cities.

Clients occasionally want to choose one partner at Gewers Pudewill, but Gewers Pudewill design all their projects together. When the architect understands exactly what is taking place in the building, the facades can respond. The B/S/H/ building is white, for example, because white goods are produced in it. The connection is not always so direct. In the case of the Carl Zeiss Meditec building >222 in Berlin, Gewers Pudewill chose a pure white facade because conditions of maximum medical hygiene are important for the work going on inside. The building should look so clean "that germs die off as soon as they get anywhere near," says Pudewill.

The *architecture parlante* ("speaking architecture") of the French Revolutionary period illustrates its functions with visual means. But that is not what the designs by Gewers Pudewill aim at. They use small and subtle allusions, rather than monocausal imagery. In their design for the Fraunhofer Institute for Ceramic Technologies and Systems (IKTS) in Hermsdorf >164, for example, Gewers Pudewill developed a parallelogram with a white ceramic facade. This facade communicates the ways of thinking of the building's users, who work with high-performance ceramics, to the outside world.

Haus des Rundfunks
Berlin
Hans Poelzig, 1931

253

In the case of Gewers Pudewill's designs, something of the inside also finds itself on the outside in a heightened and abstract artistic form, without needing to be symbolic or allegorical. Topography, terrain, light, sun, wind direction, climate, building materials and traditions are all part of the *genius loci*, the spirit of the place. The analysis of needs, on the other hand, looks for sets of rules and the logic of functions and processes.

Needs analysis as one approach, and the development of the building against the backdrop of external urban-planning constraints as the second, are not on their own sufficient for a successful design, because they suggest inevitability. The same analysis could also lead to a different result. To location or function, it is necessary to add a designer who makes a third thing out of them. The fact all the entries in a competition are different, even though the parameters are the same, is what constitutes the diversity in architecture.

An in-depth needs analysis does not lead to obligatory solutions, in other words, but it is illuminating. There is a greater probability that it will produce a satisfactory result. Prior to the design, Gewers Pudewill calmly analyze the framework conditions of the commission and establish basic principles and goals. It is not yet about solutions at this stage.

Gewers Pudewill see themselves as contextualists, but the context alone is not sufficient for their design. Only when the architects consider all the parameters does the idea follow. Gewers Pudewill take time to shape each project "out of the influences from outside, inside and from the commission itself," as they describe it. After this analysis of the fundamentals, they develop several solutions, which they test. At this point, they still have their minds fully open to all possible solutions, whereas many architects set out on a specific journey from the outset.

At Gewers Pudewill, designing is done with words, pencils and Styrodur boards. The architects think in pictures and, in the first phase, jointly develop a guiding concept that is both strong and feasible. Then comes the fine-tuning, which is an evolutionary process. "We don't announce the solution, but we have a basic agreement on the direction. We get the project on track at this time," says Henry Pudewill.

In this phase, Gewers and Pudewill work as a pair and then carry their joint design through to the end. Gewers and Pudewill take this first stage, which they call "our time," very seriously. After that, the project sits. The strength of the idea, and its viable and resilient formulation with regards to the client, the site and the commission, are already enough to carry it through to implementation. From this point on, the designers make no further interventions in the basic structures. The team is then able to develop the design in more depth and contribute fresh thoughts. This early, intensive setting of a strong vision also firmly establishes the design in the mind of the client.

House for Dr. Sternfeld
Berlin
Erich Mendelsohn, 1923

This approach recalls the words of Louis Sullivan, the father of modern architecture: "It is of the very essence of every problem that it contains and suggests its own solution." For Sullivan, form was not something preconceived or determined *a priori*, but something intrinsically present in the task in question. One generation later, Hugo Häring wrote that designing, for him, meant searching for form rather than imposing it. He thereby drew a comparison with nature, in which "form is the result of the organization of many individual entities in space, in order that life can unfold and action take place, a fulfilment of both part and whole."

Architecture should effect something, create a space. Gewers Pudewill want to design buildings that occupy people's minds.
An architecture without people, serving only itself, is not enough for Gewers Pudewill. For them, a conversion or a new building must result in something positive for the natural world or for people: knowledge gained, for example, or quality of living. Or both.

The evolution of the design

Although biology and nature bring forth magnificent, inspiring and meaningful forms, Gewers Pudewill do not take them as a design principle. Nature does not design: it produces forms of all different kinds, without being bound to schemata. Diatoms may resemble building structures in the same way as trees the supporting framework of a hall, but neither bionics nor biomimicry is central to Gewers Pudewill's designs, since the architects are also interested in social and historical contexts. Their work is not based on a theoretical foundation, but responds pragmatically to the site and the commission in question. For them, architecture is a response to the questions of how people function and what motivates them. Architecture is immersive and inescapable. It surrounds us and exerts a great influence on us. "Only when our building functions in people's daily lives, have we succeeded," say Gewers Pudewill. The two architects command an astonishingly broad portfolio of commissions, ranging from industrial and residential complexes to commercial and office premises. "I wanted to stop after the first high-rise, but then the second one came along. We let ourselves get excited over and over again," says Pudewill.

Rosario Alessandro Alessi, Songül Altindis, Oscar Robert Aporius, Jasmin Arjang, Anne Arlt, Nikos Athanasiadis, Faten Atwal, Alon Axelrod, Martino Baldassarri, Joachim Bath, Florian Baumgartner, Reiner Beelitz, Matthias Bellmann, Juliane Bernhardt, Thomas Birk, Julia Borchers, Tobias Bortolussi, Carsten Borucki, Kora Böttger, Bernd Bronnert, Philip Brüggemann, Christoph Bukowski, Veit Burgbacher, Svenja Burow, Thomas Buser, Murat Busurk, Anna Büttner, Dalia Butvidaite-Weißmehl, Carola Butze, Julian Cassirer, Giorgi Chinchaladze, Kim Clement, Janina Cornelius, Marcus Czech, Yvonne Dauz, Amirsaman Delrooz, Andrea Di Palma, Agnese Di Quirico, Christina Doll, Aymar Dower, Julia Dragoeva-Sedelies, Paul Ebell, Eva-Maria Ebner, Kaspar Ehrhardt, Hanieh Elhamiyan, Tamir Enkhtsatsral-Hoever, Katharina Esser, Markus Fengler, Jascha Fink, Julian Fissler, André Flaskamp, Elena Flegler, Anne Fortuniak, Cristina Freni, Steffi Furgol, Marcel Gallinge, Tino Gennaro, Elisa Gersdorf, Georg Gewers, Elena Ghinita, Karoline Giessler, Matthias Goetze, Florian Gottschalk, Pietro Greco, Theresa-Marie Greiwe, Ulf Griesel, Andreas Groh, Alaa Haddad, Birgit Hampel-Chikalov, Nina Hattingh, Michael Hauser, Katja Haustein, Reema Helo, Janine Henkel, Roland Herpel, Carsten Herzig, Christoph Hesse, Marcel Heyn, Matthias Hirche, Yeon Wha Hong, Till Hornawsky, Jan Hörning, Robert Hortig, Po-Chun Hsieh, Maren Hütteroth, Klaus Intrau, John Ireton, Dominica Iskra, Anastasiya Ivashchenko, Sandra Jansen, Claudius Janser, Roman Jaszczyk, Stephanie Jungwirt-Schmitt, Antje Kalus, Kristin Karig, Anna Kaufmann, George Antoine Khawam, Daniela Kinzel, Maria Köhler, Andreas König, Inna Kotel, Eftychia Kotsareli, Daniela Kötter, Lydia Kotzan, Katerina Koutentaki, Kerstin Krüger, Kevin Krüske, Peter Kühling, Kay Kulinna, Constanze Kummer, Artur Kupriichuk, Joyce Labuch, Moritz Lang, Felix Langer, Buyan Li, Annika Lindberg, Rosa Ana López Jueguen, Birgit Lösing, Caroline Lossack, Simon Lütgemeyer,

Jennifer Lutz, Sylvia Lutz, Jacek Maj, Chhayana Mann, Piotr Margiel, Samuel Arun Markus, Liron Master, Peggy Matschos, Katharina Matz, Alexander Melchior, Alexander Mendelsohn, Frank Menzel, Linda Miede, Miriam Mlecek, Giuliana Moretti, Evangelos Moulianitis, Dirk Müller, Katharina Naam, Felix Matthias Nagel, Matthis Nägele, Igor Nazarczuk, Anna Nibell, Natalia Novoa Vidal, Tim Obermann, Sofia Olofsson, Burak Onur, Türkan Öztürk, Jan Parth, Monika Pawlak, Stefan Petro, Annamaria Piccinini, Sabrina Pinkes, Paulina Pleskot, Nico Pluntke, Leon Pollack, Pauline Pommerenke, Sascha Pöschl, Paul Hans Preller, Thomas Probst, Henry Pudewill, Joost Pudewill, Beate Quaschning, Horia Racovitan, Clara Radtke, Nabil Rajjoub, Giorgi Ramishvili, Philipp Reimann, Max Rein, Tilman Richter v. Senfft, Benito Richwien, Julio Rios, Evgenij Ritt, José Manuel Rodríguez Lopéz, Nikolas Rogge, Pavel Romanov, Klaus Romberg, Jan Roth, Adriana Ruiz, Ahmed Saeed, Barbara Salazar Oyarce, Denny Sannemann, Cosima Annette Enza Saponaro, Emine Sarikaya, Maria Sasse, Oguzhan Saygi, Elisabetta Scarafone, Borislav Schalev, Anna Schatt, Lisa Schettler, Carsten Schilk, Julia Schleppe, Constantin Schmitt, Carolin Schnevoigt, Katharina Scholtisek, Jörg M. Schreiber, Alexander Schulz, Daniel Schuster, Almut Seeger, Lisa Seibert, Muchen Shen, Josep Soler Padros, Sven Schichor, Michael Spieler, Yuli Sri Hartanto, Adrian Steckeweh, Magdalena Stefanska, Josephine Stenzel, Olga Stepien, Danilo Suhrweier, Marcin Szumilas, Marlene Treheux, Konstantinos Tsimpouris, Francois Vandendriessche, Ina Vetter, Stella Volmer, Anne von Knobelsdorff, Neele von Seggern, Wolfgang Wagner, Jörn Wähnert, Karoline Walter, Jana Warnatzsch, Michaela Weiß, Jeanette Werner, Szymon Wilczyński, Philipp Winter, Ulf Wlcek, Matthias Wolff, Takyoung Woo, Oliver Wrunsch, Philipp Wüstenberg, Andrey Yordanov, Hanui Sori You, Shayan Zamani, Bojan Zdravković, Nancy Zimmermann, Meike Zimmermann, Paul Zöll

Georg Gewers thanks his wife Ekaterini
and his children Adrian and Danaë for their
patience, their support and their wonderfully
cheerful inspiration.

Henry Pudewill thanks his parents Dr. Jürgen
and Dr. Edith Pudewill, his wife Sandra, and
his sons Joost Frieder and Yann Magne for
their loving support and unwavering trust.

Imprint

Concept: Eberle & Eisfeld
Translation: Karen Williams
Design: Eberle & Eisfeld
Image processing: Eberle & Eisfeld
Printing and binding:
DZA Druckerei zu Altenburg GmbH, Thuringia

© 2023 Gewers Pudewill and
Park Books AG, Zürich

© for the texts: the authors
© for the images: see image credits

Park Books
Niederdorfstrasse 54
8001 Zürich
Switzerland
www.park-books.com

Park Books is being supported by the
Federal Office of Culture with a general
subsidy for the years 2021–2024.

All rights reserved; no part of this publication
may be reproduced, stored in a retrieval
system or transmitted in any form or by any
means, electronic, mechanical, photocopying,
recording, or otherwise, without the prior
written consent of the publisher.

ISBN 978-3-03860-352-8
German edition: ISBN 978-3-03860-335-1

Image credits

Kora Böttger: 229
Martin Eberle: 66, 68, 70, 72, 74, 76, 77, 78,
96, 98, 115, 175, 212, 221, 222, 232, 242
HGEsch: 8, 12, 14, 30, 32, 34, 36, 37, 39, 40, 45,
46, 48, 49, 50, 52, 56, 58, 60, 62, 64, 67, 81, 82, 84,
85, 86, 94, 100, 102, 104, 106, 108, 120, 122, 126,
128, 130, 132, 134, 136, 144, 147, 148, 150, 152, 154,
157, 158, 160, 162, 164, 165, 166, 167, 168, 170, 172,
174, 176, 178, 180, 182, 184, 185, 186, 188, 190, 192,
193, 194, 202, 204, 206, 207, 208, 214, 216, 217,
218, 220, 224, 230, 234, 236, 237, 238, 239, 240
Christian Gahl: 124, 228
Michel Koczy: 54
Felix Loecher: 210, 211
Peer Schroeder: 42, 80
Philipp Winter: 110, 116, 119, 250, 251,
252, 253, 254, 257, 266, 270